Camouflaged Bitterness

Masking Was Her Calling

Brittany Jenkins

Because I was sick and tired of being the enemy's pet by allowing bitterness to control my destiny, I needed to see what lay on the other side. So, I took a deep breath, looked in the mirror, and asked God to show me Brittany beneath the masks, and behind the bitterness.

Contents

Dedication

To my only child, Zaniah McDowell, thank you. Birthing you was and will always be my greatest achievement. Your existence pulled elements out of me that would have lied dormant had God not chosen you to be my seed. I pray that I make you proud today and every day. The sum total of all I am and do is to create seeds sown in you that I look forward to witnessing manifest a beautiful harvest one day. I love you without effort baby girl.

To my mother, Barbara Jenkins: I can never thank you enough for every sacrifice you made for my sister and I. My work ethic is a direct representation of what I saw growing up. You never once complained. I appreciate you more than you will ever know. I hope that I've made you proud and continue to do so. You're going to put your feet up very soon.

To my best friend, my grandmother, and the wind beneath my wings. I'm beyond grateful to be YOUR granddaughter. Thank you for being stern and calling me out of that dark place of bitterness on many occasions. Thank you for being a virtuous woman and cheering me on to becoming a woman after God's own heart. I love you.

Preface

Whelp. Here we are. Right where I imagined being for years. Procrastination got the best of me more times than I can count in pigs and in sheep. I received confirmation after confirmation, and maybe a prophecy or two. But that alone still didn't force me to finally put the pen to the paper, or fingers to the keyboard. Getting going wasn't the hard part either as I'm sure that was your initial thought.

Since childhood I've always had a way with words and have been passionate about stories that people enjoy reading. The issue was staying motivated and consistent once started. It was reprogramming my mind on many occasions to understand the concept of birthing something this massive would never be a walk in the park. In fact, it was quite the opposite. I gave birth to a natural baby and endured a horrible pregnancy and delivery. I experienced the type of pregnancy that would cause many women to never even consider conceiving another child.

Opposition seemed to come from every angle, and I do mean EVERY angle. So much so that I questioned the timing of delivering this baby far too many times, as if pressing pause on a pregnancy or an active labor was at all possible. I had actually come to terms with God saying this wasn't the season of giving birth to such a heavy pounder. Many days I was certain the devil had secret insight on the numerous thoughts in my mind concerning the breadth and width to which this book would travel and enter hearts that would ultimately begin a process of healing. It was a process he'd hope you would cancel the appointment or better yet be a no show, and that you would silence the conversations that subtly crept in your mind suggesting something wasn't quite right. I'm almost positive one of his little imps kept him in the know as to the details of this self-help novel, even down to the details of the cover. It seemed as though I was pregnant with this baby for what many know to be an elephant pregnancy.

Don't get me wrong; I expected opposition. I understand that's the breathing ground and prerequisite for a miracle to take place. But nothing close to the magnitude of which this baby yielded. It was worse than morning sickness and bad back pains combined, and far beyond swollen feet or weird cravings. I endured telling my vision to six different graphic designers before someone could understand the concept and deliver it flawlessly. Every time

I thought we were close to the perfect layout, I realized we weren't and something was missing. That "it" factor wasn't there. I could have settled and taken just anything, but I knew what this book would do for you. For me.

You know the saying "love at first sight," right? Well, I felt this download from heaven would be healing before first sight for the masses. A nauseous feeling came over me like nothing I'd ever experienced just before sending the final manuscript to the editor. Knots formed in my belly, which led to no appetite whatsoever. I didn't understand it. But I knew something was about to happen and the enemy had plans to discourage in hopes that I would throw in the towel and quit. After a while, I finally pushed through in determination of seeing what exactly was on the other side that he ultimately never wished for me to experience. In all honesty, he desired that I never even glance with my natural eyes at a piece of the promise. Not even with a magnifying glass. Then it occurred to me that I was the holdup to someone's deliverance, freedom, healing, and maybe even their survival. Wow. Rehearsing those words in my mind and even typing them out just gave me chills. You'll see why shortly.

Fortunately, for you and I, the numerous revelations God has given over the years finally made the pages of this book that now rest between the palms of your hands like that of a worshipper awaiting something from glory. I'm almost certain you will have reached the last page of this book in less than twenty-four hours, whether that was the initial plan or just by happenstance. Social media will be forced to take a back seat and even your most favorite reality television shows will have to hang with their long-time friend, DVR. There won't be a crease or folded pages. Maybe the residue of a few tears from page to page. But the good and bad tears. Either way, they were designed for such a time as this and need to be shed. So now, healing can begin. But other than that, makeup smears and wrinkled page edges won't be the case this go-around. A bookmark may even be pushing it. Oh, and by the way, this probably won't be the book you allow a close friend to borrow—especially the close friend that never seems to return anything. It was manufactured just for you, your tears, your insecurities, and your plea for help. I suggest you apologize in advance because they will certainly need their own copy.

Oftentimes, the frequency between God and I had been a little choppy to say the least. I can be transparent for a moment in saying it was mostly on my part. Wait, it was all on my part. Truth is, He never moved, but somehow my position and posture created distance and resistance between the two of us. I wanted to hear from Him, but I wasn't always mature enough to receive that which He said. I heard a preacher once call it the power of posture. On the other hand, I always managed to get my issues in the ear of my friends before God plenty of times. Some days I didn't care to listen anyway. Even further, I didn't always make time to hear His voice though social media and reality TV always made the cut, especially the latter.

Isn't it funny how we can be mature in one area of our lives and like that of an infant in others? We can be wise in one area and a fool in the other. My flesh wanted justification in my feelings of why the steps toward my destiny were not swift but sometimes sluggish if not nonexistent at times. Whether the title or design of this cover prompted you to be even the slightest bit intrigued, I am happy you're HERE. And since we're being honest, I'll be your new best friend as you journey through this book.

I'm sure your childhood bestie will be okay with this change being as though it's not permanent.

Smile. I can imagine how much the enemy wanted to fight or even distract you from making this purchase. You may have even logged into your checking account online to see if the purchase agreed with the numbers reflected in the available balance. I'm convinced he wanted to bully you into believing that small seed of bitterness you've carried longer than a full-term baby, which might even be a root at this point, was okay to have. I know about bullying all too well. He's had a chain around my neck for years. Well, up until recently. I can almost hear him whispering in your ear many days that you have a right to feel what you feel toward whomever or whatever. The incident which led to offense could be as recent as three hours ago or even decades.

He's probably gone as far as writing on a mirror in your favorite Ruby Woo lipstick, "You are just fine." When in reality, you are slowly dying from this dis-ease that wishes to rob you of any joy now and definitely in the future. You see bitterness has never been loud and obnoxious. She's always been a slow, silent killer. To be honest, he doesn't quite like the idea of someone speaking to things you wished to remain hidden, especially since you've managed to disguise it well for years now. Not to mention helping you on the journey towards FREEDOM. Silly rabbit. He's still defeated.

Not only am I happy you're here, I'm more grateful that something in you chose to set pride aside for your next breakthrough that's bound to happen after completion of this work. Whether it's voluntarily or involuntarily. The journey you and I are about to embark on isn't so delightful to say the least. It may be a little difficult at times—even painful—as you identify and root out areas of deception that have held you in a place of bondage for longer than you can remember. It was easy for the Bible to reference "mountain be removed." But a root, that's a whole different giant you may not have been prepared or equipped to defeat. Or perhaps, you didn't possess the proper ammunition to fight effectively. Better late than never right?

One of the hardest concepts of getting healed and ultimately whole, is self-evaluation in admitting there is an issue. A heart issue. I can't say that you won't need heart surgery after completing the final page. But I submit to you today that I know the ultimate heart surgeon whose resume is flawless and a backup plan is never needed. His nature of omnipotence affords Him the ability to perform the surgery, clean up in the most sanitary way possible, and hold you in comfort before you even awaken from the numbness. He is THAT type of God. I call him J-E-S-U-S.

Throughout the next few chapters I'll be discussing several different stories about different women with different situations who just so happen to have the same deep issue: *bitterness*. You may relate to one or all of their circumstances. Regardless of the match, bitterness is real and doesn't discriminate. She quietly seeps into areas of our lives we never imaged with no invitation. So, *beware*.

Your famine of bitterness will never be the same again. Brace yourself; it's time to circumcise the fleshly part of you that's been hindering your growth, preventing you from reaching your maximum and consequently polluting your future. It's the pollution that we've now identified as *bitterness*.

Define It

Let all bitterness, and wrath, and anger, and clamor, and evil speaking, be put away from you, with all malice:
(Ephesians 4:31-32)(KJV)

Looking diligently lest any man fail of the grace of God; lest any root of bitterness springing up trouble [you], and thereby many be defiled; (Hebrews 12:15)(KJV)

***

Cam·ou·flage

[kam-uh-flahzh]

Noun

1. the act, means, or result of obscuring things to deceive an enemy, as by painting or screening objects so that they are lost to view in the background.

Bit·ter·ness

'bidərnəs/

Noun

1. A feeling of deep and bitter anger and ill-will. A feeling of sulky resentment. A resentment strong enough to justify retaliation.

Define it. As if that's necessary right? Truthfully speaking, something on the inside prompted you to even reach and grab this book, let alone go to check out and spend your coins on a novel that quite possibly will step on your toes. And yes, even toes you never knew existed. Don't worry, I won't judge. It's actually impossible to judge when I was once in your position. Quite frankly, some days I'm still there. How so, you ask? Because bitterness is a CHOICE. Oftentimes, I chose her, not for once realizing the magnitude of the customizable consequences that would follow and try to torment my childhood and adult life. The residue of bitterness some days splatters my face like that of an infant seconds away from demolishing their favorite meal of spaghetti.

I would take camouflaged bitterness as being the art of hiding that which is slowly killing you behind closed doors, in a dark room without a single window. Grabbing your neck and choking you with no sign of release. You never signed up for the course but somehow passed with flying colors. Camouflaged bitterness prevents one from celebrating exciting moments for others, because of issues one may be facing inwardly. It's like a roadblock where one is forced to exit the vehicle even after a license and registration are presented, mainly because other harmful items may or may not be loaded in the trunk of the car. Camouflaged bitterness is that knotty, stomach feeling which stems from anxiety and anger as one continues to hold onto past hurt. It's the fake smile one must disguise in order to blend in with the mass majority who are seemingly smiling genuinely. It's the quick response of "I'm doing great, thank you for asking" when someone asks how are you. It's often displayed by interjecting comments of self in conversations intended to shine a light on others. It's shown behind false smiles hiding dozens of emotions waiting to finally resume to one's normal disposition. It's pretending to be ok with your current state when in fact you're still miserable from past hurt.

Customarily, we see camouflage attire worn by members of armed forces or hunters. People wear camouflage to hide themselves from the enemy in most instances. In 1992, a landmark study took place that attempted to figure out exactly what deer see. The results show that deer are red-green colorblind. What this means is that deer can tell the difference between blue from red, but not green from red, or orange from red. Therefore, hunters can wear green, red, or orange and blend right in, but should stay away from blue.* Taking a look at this theory further, if one camouflages themselves to look like others, the chance of bitterness being seen by those among them is pretty slim. We tend to camouflage with our wardrobe, our degrees, our houses and cars, our makeup and hair preferences, our speech, and even our associations.

Masking was always the better option as opposed to confronting the issue head on. I became a professional at hiding this infirmity better than I had the strength of looking "it" in the eye and pronouncing death for that which wanted to kill me. Bitterness can often cause one to wonder why it wasn't happening for them when those it was happening for didn't appear to be as qualified. Of course you could tend to whatever "it" is better than they could, right? If bitterness was hiring, I managed to beat out any and all candidates applying for the position before the posting ever made the employer's website. Did your resume also get forwarded to the employer?

Perhaps you're still in a place of denial. In your mind, it's just anger that will eventually go away once you decide to come to terms with what "they" did. I too tried to convince myself that my feelings weren't deep enough to be considered bitterness. It was just a little anger, right? Truth is, anger is usually a short-lived reaction while bitterness lingers around for a while with no plans or agenda of leaving. It latches with no desire of letting go. Anger doesn't last forever. Some people cope by going to the gym, taking a long walk, or even forcing themselves to sleep. I find that when I'm angry, I can typically cool off at least by the next day depending on the situation, or after venting to granny. But honestly, I look back and wonder if it was even worth the attention or energy. But in the moment, I had a right to feel what I feel. One thing for sure, I allowed anger to turn into bitterness, and that bitterness grew almost exponentially. I wanted revenge, whether I initiated it or God took care of it.

Bitterness keeps us from being happy. It's festering anger. I've learned that anger I can control, but bitterness had a way of yanking me around and controlling me to do what "it" wanted me to do. It kept me from moving on and from moving ahead. Bitterness tends to lead to resentment and ultimately, you find yourself holding a grudge. Hold a grudge and lose a miracle. Sadly, I happened to be the queen of holding grudges for years. Once anyone wronged me, best believe walls went up immediately. And let's not even mention if it was intentional or avoidable. Yeah, your name went on a "no contact" list in my mind. There was absolutely no way I would even give you the opportunity to hurt or wrong me for the second time. As they say, if I cut you off, chances are, you gave me the scissors. Like an immature adult, I blamed my ex for making me so stubborn. Rest assured that bitterness is silent. I didn't have to tell them they wronged me or that I had no intentions of ever dealing with them again. Oh, but when I was angry, you may or may not have seen a subliminal Facebook post about it. I could definitely get in the ring of pettiness with the best of them.

Have you ever seen anyone mask anger? Nope, me either. Angry people will make sure everyone knows they're angry. But bitterness is certainly more internal. It quietly festers, making sure to not disturb the peace to the point that it's noticeable. I wallowed in my pool of bitterness and no one ever knew. Well, except for my granny.

As you can see, and probably already knew, bitterness is like no other emotion one can feel. The only difference is the way in which it's hidden. Have you too learned the best practices of camouflaging your bitterness?

Abandoned Property

A father to the fatherless (Psalm 68:5)(KJV)

When my father and my mother forsake me, then the Lord will take me up. (Psalm 27:10)(KJV)

***

n. property left behind (often by a tenant) intentionally and permanently when it appears that the former owner (or tenant) does not intend to come back, pick it up, or use it.

***

Five dollars.

One.

Two.

Three.

Four.

Five.

Five measly dollars. Even as a toddler, she knew that couldn't amount to much. But that's what Tiffany remembered receiving from her dad when they crossed paths at the local carwash every blue moon. Come to think about it, he probably had more money than the owners of that rundown local hang out. To some, five dollars may seem grand to a child who probably couldn't count past one hundred. But when your dad was one of the biggest local drug dealers, five dollars was tacky; it was never enough and NEVER would be. But more importantly, it was enough for her to understand she didn't matter to him one bit.

Her mama couldn't file for child support if she wanted to since proving his income was nearly impossible. He seemed to always be posted up with his boys. It was the same boys that had no intentions of ever holding him accountable to being a real father and a real man in a community where African American men were already stereotyped with negative misconceptions. They were the same boys that didn't mind keeping him in the streets because going home to his child(ren) was never on his top five of things to do. To be honest, those same boys probably also had children by multiple women they were neglecting as well. Birds of a feather typically do flock together. But for them, they were hanging with the top dog. He was the best of the best when it came to slanging drugs.

Tiffany learned at a young age that age had nothing to do with maturity because her father was one of the most child-like adults she had ever met. Going through her younger years, she never had the choice of answering questions about her father in the classroom setting. She had no idea of his highest level of education, his birthday, age, or even middle name. On the contrary, her mother's information was memorized, even her social security number. Unfortunately and fortunately, she wouldn't have the chance of knowing since he had been taken into custody and finally behind bars on felony charges.

Days turned into months, and months into years. Before she knew it, her father was behind bars up until her high school years. This was her normal and all she ever knew was mommy played two roles and worked hours that suggested so. Ironically, all of her dearest and close friends growing up each had their fathers in the home. Tiffany couldn't help but live her life and desire to have a loving father through her friends. Numerous days she witnessed her best friends being picked up by their fathers from school and the Boys & Girls Club, only imagining what the conversations were like with a male once they stepped foot in the car.

In high school, she questioned God and His decision of positioning her around friends who had what she yearned for. More often than not, she felt as though His choice in doing so was tied to her hurt. She hadn't fully matured to understanding His nature and agape love for His children. All she could see was an empty glass. It was never even half full in her eyes though she had a mother who worked earnestly to make up the slack and shield her from emotions that surfaced before she could get rid of them. Her mother worked twelve to fourteen-hour days, six and seven days a week to ensure that her girls received the same love, attention, and benefits children who lived in two-parent homes had.

Tiffany's senior year of high school happened to be the year of release for her father from prison. She hadn't thought much about it since her life had been shaped and molded around the disappointing reality of having one parent. That's all she knew. Later in life she realized that's all she needed. Small talk around town about her father being released forced emotions to flare up that she wasn't ready to deal with. For once, Tiffany wondered what it would be like to have 'Dad' registered on the caller-ID of her cell phone. What did it feel like having a man outside of her uncle and grandfather saying, "I love you"? She wondered if he would try to make up for lost time and take her on father/daughter dates like she was coerced to lust after growing up. Would they spend time together on the weekends when she wasn't at work or spending time with her boyfriend?

Thousands of thoughts ran through her mind that she actually never anticipated having. The only thing she knew to do was what she always did. Write. Tiffany began writing down all of her thoughts and feelings in a journal that she would one day transfer in a letter to give to him once they met. She was always good with words and felt this was the best way to release everything that had kept her mind hostage. It was her way of being honest, withholding nothing. Over the years it was never foreign to hear from numerous people that she looked just like her dad. She had only seen pictures and never had a clear picture in her head of how he looked as visiting him in prison was out of the question. She only spoke with him one time during the eight-year duration he was locked up. She could only recall one time speaking with him and that was by accident when his mother asked her to answer the phone one random day she happened to be visiting. For all

Tiffany knew, she didn't look much like her mother so she had to be a splitting image of her dad.

The day had come and her mother arranged to take Tiffany to her dad's grandmother's house where he would be staying. This wasn't his initial day of being released but that was okay with Tiffany. Her appetite was non-existent at this point. She was about to meet a stranger who happened to be her dad. He was never mailed spring pictures of her over the years so he couldn't possibly know what to expect either. They were likely in the same position of nervousness, but being as though Tiffany was female, her emotions were times ten. Though Tiffany was approaching seventeen, she wished her mom could stay with her. Fortunately and unfortunately, this was something Tiffany had to face alone.

For whatever reason, it seemed as though they reached her great grandmother's home in seconds. Tiffany's palms were soaking wet at this point. Why was she so nervous to meet the man who was part responsible for her existence? The fact that "meeting" him was a terminology used saddened her even the more. This wasn't the way it was supposed to be. He should be the man of her life, keeping her from dating any low lives. He should be the man who she ran to for comfort, and the man who did so well validating her essence of queendom that another "boy" would never have to do so. He was supposed to be the man who sent flowers and huge cards to the school every year for Valentine's Day as an example for any boy bold enough to date his daughter. He was supposed to be the man with a nice .45 gun on his side that threatened any boy who decided to keep his daughter out past her curfew or didn't think it necessary to knock on the door and meet him and her mother.

So many thoughts of who he should have been raced through her mind. This felt like something seen on a movie rather than her real life experience. Tiffany finally got the nerve to get out of the car after pleading and begging her mother to bring her back another day. Either that or her mom could just come in with her this one time. Her mother was forced to just about push her out the car so Tiffany had no choice but to make her way to the front door. Surprisingly, her great grandmother greeted her on the porch, which actually helped calm her just a little.

She was the sweetest little lady with the most beautiful grey hair and high-pitched voice. They hugged and her great grandmother yelled for her dad to come to the living room. He knew Tiffany was on her way so one would think after eight years he would have been waiting in the driveway for her with excitement. Tiffany heard him coming down the hall slowly. At this point, her stomach was in more knots than a bucket of hair bows collected for three little girls over the years. She remained standing to give him a hug once he made it down the hall. Maybe a handshake would have actually been more appropriate. If there was a book on the first time experience of meeting your father as a teenager, Tiffany would have certainly checked it out from the local library and kept it longer than the time allotted. Again, none of her friends had a similar background so she had no one to rely on for advice of what to expect.

Ironically, he had this slothful demeanor and lackadaisical presence that Tiffany didn't appreciate. Since she knew nothing much about him aside from his name, knowing what to make of his presence was pretty impossible. One thing for sure, this would be a long night of venting with granny and a few new pages in her journal the minute she stepped in her home that evening.

Her dad finally made it to the living room area after what seemed like decades. They hugged for what could be described as a "church" hug and preceded to the couch. Tiffany's great grandmother must have made an exit to her room the moment their arms raised for the not so normal hug. Tiffany surely wasn't pleased with that. Gratefully, she left the TV on with a low volume, which would act as Tiffany's escape in avoiding eye contact or too much conversation with her dad. As much as Tiffany was uncomfortable with this awkward experience, she could tell her dad was the same if not more.

He seemed to pay more attention to the soap opera than Tiffany did. He asked the basic questions as though he wasn't sure of what else to possibly say. How is school, do you have a boyfriend, and why she never visited him in prison to name a few. Tiffany answered with the shortest amount of words possible. By this point she tried to prevent her attitude from being visible as she spoke. Her great grandmother was still in the back room with the door closed.

In Tiffany's eyes, this was the perfect opportunity for him to apologize for every important event leading up to then he had missed in her life. This was the perfect time for him to ask what she needed materialistically and emotionally. Here was the chance for him to promise quality time and arrange for them to hang out and get to know one another better. Father/daughter dates could actually be a reality for Tiffany and not something she only saw displayed amongst her close friends. This was the perfect time for him to assure her that his absence or inactivity in her life was merely a thing of the past and today would start a fresh day of new beginnings.

She wasn't expecting tears to be shed but that actually suited the timing given the circumstance. Besides, not having him as a part of her life over the years was certainly not something to take lightly. He never apologized or allowed words to leave his lips that would cause Tiffany to believe he was even the least bit resentful for his non-involvement in her life. And one day, Tiffany would accept just that with no other explanation needed. She knew deep down she never did a single thing to cause him not to desire a genuine relationship with her, and that's all she needed to know. Tiffany didn't understand then, but growing up in a single parent home would work for her good. It was all a part of God's plan to bring her to a predestined end.

Before she knew it, her mother was headed back to pick her up. From her short visit, it was easy for Tiffany to gather that if anything was to come from her relationship with her dad, he would have to step up as the parent and make it clear that he desired to know her just as much as she did if not more. Cycles, which never led anywhere, seemed to be the perfect way to describe their relationship. Broken promises after broken promises. It seemed to be more of a "situationship" that eventually grew pointless at one point for Tiffany.

This little girl needed her father to be the mature adult for once. To step up and act as though he helped bring her into existence and wasn't on the same level as his child. Let's be quite frank, how in the world did God choose her to be a bastard child out of many? Not only that, but He surrounded Tiffany with friends who lived in two-parent homes knowing that envy and bitterness would take root. And in her case, let's just say it sprouted into a full-grown oak tree. It's one thing to not know your father and never have a true relationship with him from birth or childhood, but it's another to know him but also know he doesn't care about an authentic relationship with you. And you know what Tiffany never understood, was how the same absent fathers ended up with the most women?

As women, one would think coming together in solidarity against no good men would be ideal. Instead, some women preferred to share beds, amongst other things, with worthless men. Tiffany could never imagine being intimate or having any type of dealings with a man who wasn't active and involved in his child(ren's) life. Talk about a huge turnoff. His ability to nurture and grow relationships with women, and their children, but disregard her existence as his child contributed to a bitter heart that had no intentions of forgiving or making something beautiful out of nothing. She was fed up. And we all know what happens when a woman's fed up.

Punk, coward, and childish were just a few names that came to mind any time his name or an image of him crossed her mind once Tiffany decided she was done with entertaining a relationship with him. All he seemed to possess was cowardice tendencies. She was amazed that the four walls of the prison and other inmates who committed hard knock crimes didn't harden him just a little or cause him to even desire making his wrongs right. Though his appearance still showed that of a weak man she assumed for sure he would have some sort of backbone after several years in the pen.

Regrettably, she assumed it was the parent's responsibility to be the parent. He was supposed to be the man who showed her what love from a real man was like far before any "boy" could trick her into a false love spell. He was designed by God to be the father who showered her with love and protected her from any danger that was avoidable. He was supposed to be the provider. He was supposed to tell her how valuable and worthy she was daily to the point where it was annoying and embarrassing for her. He was supposed to be the man she ran home to and laid on his chest with tears streaming down her face after the little mixed boy, who wore the hottest and trendiest clothes, in first grade kicked her at recess as an immature sign of his crush on her. He was supposed to be the father that waited all week in anticipation for the father/daughter dance. He should have showed up to some of her piano recitals or step shows.

Some men had no clue how to be a father. He was one of them. Some would argue to say this might be the case since most men never had fathers in their own lives to be the example. But this was an excuse Tiffany despised hearing. Everyone has choices and a clear mind of what's right and wrong. Somewhere along the way, the roles reversed and she was the parent while her dad mastered traits, characteristics, and responsibilities of a child to a "t". Only prayer and a miracle could reverse the curse and switch the roles back to the way God intended.

Tiffany was the property and her dad was the tenant. He left. And now we have 'abandoned property'. She was trippin' over a man who could not care less of the calling on her life, not realizing the blessing in disguise. God blessed her with a grandfather and uncle who would drop whatever they were doing, at any given moment, to come and see about her when she needed manly hands. Moving furniture, oil changes, flat tires, purchase of a new car, and even a ride home from work on his motorcycle at ten o'clock at night. God had her back and sides from the day she was born. And when uncle and papa Butch couldn't come through, God would step in as the father she grew to love. His love was second to none. Despite the fact she couldn't see or feel Him physically, she could feel His spirit surrounding her.

Tiffany chose to entertain relationships she had no business entertaining while trying to fill a void her father should have owned as a child. Oddly enough, men years older than her had a way of showing interest in various ways. One of them in particular claimed he never saw a young woman with the drive and ambition Tiffany possessed. And for various reasons, she connected with others at least five years older than herself. Tiffany was certain there were other women he could easily engage in a relationship with. It was flattering of course but not enough to persuade Tiffany in dating a man her father's age just because he wasn't a part of her childhood. God allowed the void to see how she would fill it.

She heard Bishop T.D. Jakes and Steve Harvey reference countless times that forgiveness is not for the offender, but it's for you. Hmmmmmm. Right. She could never imagine this to be true being as though she would never be in a place of ever needing forgiveness if they hadn't done what they did. Why did she need forgiveness as the victim? Something wasn't right about this equation and she wasn't interested in a tutor or extra homework to understand it any further.

Rather than try to understand what it was about herself that prevented her father from desiring a genuine, loving relationship with her, Tiffany finally gave up the idea of something that wasn't realistic and focused on things she could control. And that was her relationship with herself, her relationship with God, and a healthy relationship with the man God would eventually lead to come and find her. Not concerning himself with his child was a loss on his part and Tiffany became content with just that. Did she understand it? Absolutely not. But negative energy and heartache didn't and never would usher her closer to her destiny and customized success God had just for her.

She refused to forfeit the blessings while trying to piece back a shattered glass. Besides, not having a real father in her life made her to be the woman many grew to admire. She had such a visible anointing and vowed to let her light shine no matter the situation. She vowed to be led by the spirit and not by her wounds. She was a queen. Phenomenally.

Morning Sickness

*And we know that all things work together for good to them
that love God, to them who are the called according to his purpose.
(Romans 8:28)(KJV)*

*The Lord says, "I will give you back what you lost
to the swarming locusts, the hopping locusts,
the stripping locusts, and the cutting locusts. (Joel 2:25)(NLT)*

*Brethren, I count not myself to have apprehended: but this one
thing I do, forgetting those things which are behind, and reaching forth
unto those things which are before. (Philippians 3:13)(KJV)*

"Don't do it, Syd; it's really not worth it. If my
opinion ever held any weight in your life, trust me on this
one and hear me out. I wish I could go back and keep
mine," Mallory said.

She was referring to that thing that seemed small
while one had it, but HUGE once gone. The thing the world
believed to be the determining factor of a girl turned
woman. She was talking about her virginity. Sydney had
been dating a guy just three years older and fell head over
heels for him within weeks. She was one of few virgins left
in a small school and was itching to cross over to the side
of those who had "given it up".

For whatever reason, losing your virginity equated to those who were more popular. It wasn't even that the guy was super attractive, muscular, or possessed enough coins to treat her anywhere she wanted. The thought of finally being "taken" soothed her soul like that of Vicks vapor rub to a congested toddler. The enemy had an interesting way of making younger girls feel as if their very being didn't have much value if someone wasn't itching to be close to them in a physical form primarily. In essence, she settled to be "with" someone not fully understanding that this belief didn't actually mean being "with" someone. Not realizing the tailored specific consequences her decisions would yield later in life. And when I say later, I mean a lot sooner than she imagined. Sydney was accepted into a college in Georgia just a few short weeks after they began dating. Though sad, he invited her to dinner to celebrate a huge accomplishment.

Derrick's little red Dodge Neon pulled into the driveway to pick up his date like any other day. He texted Sydney's phone and she came out dressed classy, per usual. Her glow may have been a bit brighter this day. For one particular reason I'm sure. Dinner was awkward to say the least. She never finished any of her meals when he took her out. But today, in particular, the jittery feeling in her stomach didn't come from her recent accomplishment or shy feeling of dating someone older. This day, the jittery feeling in the pit of her stomach came from knowing she was about to give away the most sacred part of her being to a guy that was furthest from being worthy of having it. And this guy, would soon be the father of her child.

Derrick wasn't the most popular guy in the city, and neither was he the most attractive. He was a typical guy who played sports in high school that made his way to being "known" by many. He had a job and car but still lived home with his mother. But Sydney heard of him being a good guy who spoiled his women with gifts and attention. At this point, she could use a whole lot of that in her life.

***

"I did it."

This was the text message Mallory received around six thirty-eight the night Sydney and her boyfriend went to celebrate her acceptance to Clark Atlanta University. Mallory shook her head in disbelief while staring at the small Cingular device that displayed this news. Surely, her friend trusted her enough to not do something so regretful. Although they were the same age, Mallory had come to terms with her immaturity and the self-condemnation associated with making adult decisions as a teenager. But now, she felt the same heartache she knew her friend would soon have to endure.

There was something about a girl dating an older "boy" that forced her to believe safety and stability would be hers now and forever. She had no idea. Like any other pleasure to flesh, Sydney found that fornication was now something she enjoyed. Or maybe she enjoyed it to the extent of believing since it pleased Derrick, it would make her enjoy it. There were a number of times she didn't "feel" like being intimate with her first love, but sucked it up and undressed anyway. Regrettably, the world made her believe this was the only way to keep him. Oh, but the day would come where God would reveal false carnal doctrine and she would be saved by His amazing grace.

Do something for twenty-one days straight and you'll program your mind to now do so habitually, says the world. Be that as it may, Sydney did not sleep with her newly found love for twenty-one days straight. Yet, the intimacy they shared was enough to shove her into the "in love" coma. It grew daily even when it wasn't fed breakfast, lunch, and dinner. She was a senior in high school and he was already introduced to the world of working being three years older. Getting to know one another consisted of full day texting sessions as she pretended to pay attention in class and phone calls on his way to work. Surprisingly, she still managed a decent grade point average and honor roll. What she failed miserably in was discernment from God concerning a relationship she probably never should have engaged in. Then, she didn't understand the capacity and chastisement that came from an unequally yoked relationship. It didn't always mean dating a non-believer. In her case, it simply meant engaging with a person outside of the will of God.

Her prayer life and intimate time with God was placed on the back burner as she focused on getting to know her new boo. Surely, God would understand since He sent Derrick. Right? Wrong. In her mind, they would have that happily ever after story to tell and she could be one from her class that met the love of their life in high school. Nights of going to bed listening to the top nine hits at eight o'clock on the local radio show turned into long nights of small talk and excitement as she anticipated the next text message. And of course, he had a ringtone that matched his contact name full of love emoji's. Sydney's school started later than other local high schools in the area so she began a normal routine of going to visit Derrick just before making it to school prior to the tardy bell ringing. On special days, she made it a point to stop by his mom's place before heading to work that afternoon.

She couldn't get enough of him. At one point, Derrick had a roommate, which made any type of intimacy a little awkward for Sydney. Nevertheless, he made up for it and ushered her into a place of total relaxation while in his presence. Because she yielded her body to him, this wasn't too hard to accomplish. She felt as though giving of herself sexually was something he "needed" as someone older, so giving just that was their normal. While most other senior girls were focused on the top football or basketball stars, Sydney tooted her own horn a bit being that her guy was older with a weekly pay that afforded him to spoil her a little more than cafeteria lunch.

Months went by and she continued to submit her body to this guy in hopes of their bond growing closer since college was just around the corner for her. In her mind, if she gave him what most boys wanted, this would keep his mind focused on her while she was away concentrating on furthering her education. As if any girl walking couldn't give him the same. Surely he would remain faithful to her since he admitted he'd never had a love like theirs before. Sydney became good at hiding her cheating ways while in the presence of family or at church. Never did she cheat on Derrick with a single guy, but God definitely witnessed her infidelity with Him. There were days she visualized God with tears in His eyes as He watched her being used in a way He knew she would later regret.

Grace could only take her but so far. She was out of the will of God, which usually forfeits His ultimate protection. Sadly, Sydney felt since other friends her age who had been sexually active much longer than her hadn't gotten pregnant, she was safe. STDs were never even a thought because she trusted Derrick. Even knowing he had been with dozens of girls before her, she trusted him. Her body belonged to God and one day soon he would reclaim the deed on that which is titled to Him until her God appointed husband came and changed that.

Summer was coming to an end which meant Sydney's first semester of college was approaching much sooner than she and Derrick preferred. She was certainly a little nervous to be away from family and friends. Besides a two-week trip to Germany, a few summer camps, and working with the Senators over the summer, she had never really been away from home. Only she and another classmate from high school were beginning their higher education journey in Georgia. Sydney and Derrick tried to spend as much time together as possible in hopes of making the transition a lot easier to bear. With that, Sydney didn't refrain from giving of herself since he wouldn't be getting it as often for at least four years. At this point, "I love you" had made its way into the ending of their phone calls or dialogue just after they kissed when departing from one another.

Derrick coming to visit at least once a month, preferably twice, was just as good as signed and sealed on paper. He made her believe they would be even closer once she departed and he would be faithful to her. She trusted that since she had high hopes of her first being her last. Ideally, her children would hear stories of their father being their mother's one and only. She cherished that goal with every ounce of her being. It was more than possible to manifest. Because Sydney had half-sisters, she vowed for such a word to not be part of her children's lives.

While pretty confident, Sydney always felt self-conscious about one thing—her smile. She could dress her behind off and her stylist made it a point to keep her hair worthy of compliments from her peers. Unfortunately, the good Lord decided to give her one too many teeth, which contributed to a crowded mouth and not so pretty smile. Before going off to college, Sydney decided to get this under control and behind her once and for all. Besides, being in a new city full of new faces, she wanted to make the best possible impression. Her mother's insurance provided a yearly amount toward orthodontic care and Sydney planned to put a hefty chunk down with her private loan money.

She made a consultation with a highly recommended orthodontist to get the process going. Terrified, Sydney was told she would need to have three teeth extracted before braces could be put on. After all the dental work she had over the years, this was certainly disappointing news. Nevertheless, Sydney was determined to have a smile she was no longer insecure about. Derrick's job wouldn't permit him accompanying her to this appointment, but her mom ended her work shift early to be there. The pain was unbearable for quite a while to say the least.

Following the appointment, all Sydney wanted was to be held by Derrick. Her mom gave him a call and he came right over immediately after his last truck stop. She was such a big baby and he knew it. As he held her, she was grateful to have a man in her life to love on her even after her father's absence. Her uncle and grandfather were always available for manly duties, but Derrick covered the love portion. Or was it disguised lust? Hmmmmmmmm. The results of that notion would soon be discovered.

Days following that terrible dentist visit, Sydney was scheduled to have her braces put on. The excitement of a new set of pearly whites soon vanished several hours after her mind understood what had just taken place. Derrick came over that day as normal and chuckled after witnessing how different their kisses would be for the next two and a half years. He always felt her smile was beautiful. Although he voiced this often with his lips, she wanted to tackle once and for all this insecurity that harassed her most of her childhood and young adult years.

The day had come and it was time to make rounds to see all family members just before heading up the highway. Sydney hadn't had her monthly cycle just yet but her grandmother assured her it was probably due to all the stress associated with leaving family and setting sail for unfamiliar territory. It had been a few weeks since she and Derrick were intimate, so pregnancy was definitely not an option. So she thought. Derrick wasn't able to travel with Sydney and her family to Georgia. So he made sure to stay over late the night before. And, he had already made plans to visit her in two weeks and book a room in close proximity of her college.

Saying goodbye to her great grandmother and uncle was a lot harder than she had imagined. Her best friend also known as her grandmother prayed a prayer that almost made Sydney reconsider this whole out-of-state college experience. She dried her tears, said her goodbyes, and hopped in the SUV with a heavy heart. Why must one be forced to grow up so fast? It seemed like just yesterday she was a freshman trying her hardest to fit in and make the oh so popular step team. Now, she was in love with a guy who lived miles away and she would be forced to mature in new ways.

Before check-in, her family decided to grab a bite to eat at the nearest Waffle House. It was at the table exchanging laughs and passing syrup that Sydney began to doubt her decisions. Not to mention, the private student loan check to pay for housing was being mailed to her home address back in North Carolina and her mom was forced to drive back.

"I could always come home and attend another Historically Black College in the next city. This way, I'll be closer to family and won't have to endure the pain of a long distance relationship with Derrick," Sydney explained to her family.

Being as though granny wasn't ready to let go of her oldest grandchild, this statement actually sounded ideal. Let's just forget that she co-signed for the private loan and took time away from work to move Sydney in. They finished up lunch and headed to the school to begin orientation prior to moving everything in her suite. Based on introductions and icebreakers, Sydney decided to befriend other females who had boyfriends back at home. If anything, they had one thing in common. For the most part, they had been with their boyfriends for many years, which meant Sydney was in good company.

It was morning, and they slept the night away. Well, maybe for Derrick. Sydney wasn't interested in sleep after counting the days before she'd be in the arms of her lover again. They had never spent more than a couple of days separated, so this transition to college had been a difficult one to say the least. Her body had grown used to being used by Derrick. She could sleep on his way home. She needed enough loving to carry over for the next few weeks and make up for this love deficit she'd been struggling with. Or was it a lust deficit? He had unspoken plans of touring the city while visiting Sydney. To their surprise, an evening at dinner ended sooner than expected after Sydney felt more and more nauseous just glancing at food on their table. Not to mention, the constant walking by with food from various servers.

He was a little upset but yielded to her wishes of going back to the hotel. She took advantage of more quality time since his visit would be over at the snap of one's fingers. If cable wasn't included in the price per night, that would have been just peachy. Sydney had no intentions of being entertained by a single channel during Derrick's last night in town. He noticed she'd been dropping weight as they bathed together. He assured her that possibilities of being pregnant were false. The stash of maxi pads she'd purchased prior to moving in her dorm still hadn't been touched. For all the two of them knew, her body was still getting adjusted to life away from home and couldn't take on a monthly cycle plus that type of stress at the moment. In addition, her appetite was forced to change drastically as she wasn't permitted to eat the same foods as prior to getting braces put on.

One hot Atlanta morning while walking to class, something didn't feel the same. Something was happening inwardly that Sydney had never felt before to even describe to her closest girlfriends. Her roommate, whenever home, walked in to see Sydney throwing up in small grocery bags from the nearest corner store. It must be this "new" heat, Sydney thought. It was always said that Georgia had a different kind of humidity; it was nothing to be played with to say the least. She made up her mind that she could cope with the sickness just a few more days since her auntie and mama would be down to pick her up for the Labor Day break. For all Derrick knew, she was good. As in not pregnant good.

The drive from Clark Atlanta to North Carolina seemed to have doubled in time with the way Sydney felt.

Not to mention they had to do a U-turn after realizing a wrong turn was made at some point. More than a crack in the window was needed if it meant Sydney made it back to her mother's house alive. She felt as though she was dying or close enough to it. After what seemed like an eternity, they finally pulled in the driveway and Sydney couldn't wait to sleep in her old bed once again. Though granny did an outstanding job making her part of the suite look "homey," it was nothing like being back at her real "home". Sydney jumped out just before the car came to a complete stop and ran in the house where her sister was the only one home at the time.

  That Sunday morning just before heading to church, Sydney's mother hurt her back while bending over too fast in the bathroom. After church they agreed the both of them would go to the nearest emergency room just five minutes from their home church so both of them could be seen and finally embark on the road to "normal" again. Sydney's great auntie called on her to pray just before church let out. She cried out to God in front of her closest relatives with not a care in the world that the doctor's wouldn't say she had some sort of food poisoning. Sydney was convinced her illness was a result of finally eating at the school diner. After all, she did go to school in Atlanta.

As they walked through the automatic doors of the Kings Mountain ER, Sydney quickly informed the front desk associate that she and her mother both needed to be seen. The wait time was typical for a weekend day but Sydney just wanted to know what it was that had her body so discombobulated. They took their seats and scrolled through social media as they waited for their names to be called.

Shortly thereafter, a nurse summoned for Sydney to have her vitals and temperature taken. She knew the nurse was required to ask when her most recent menstrual cycle was. Sadly, she couldn't remember. "Any chances you could be pregnant?" came next. Before she could even think, her mouth shouted absolutely not as though her and Derrick hadn't been intimate recently. But the nurse didn't need to know that. After her vitals were all complete, and a urine sample was given, Sydney and the nurse began walking toward a room. During this time, she saw her mother also heading toward a room on the opposite end of the hallway so their time at the hospital was just about over.

After what seemed like eternity, the door of the

cold, temporary room slowly opened and in walked the doctor. After the usual commonalities were over, the doctor's next words must have been a part of Sydney's dream. Better yet nightmare. "Well, you're pregnant, Miss Lady. Would you like me to tell your mom or are you okay telling her?"

Sydney's life came to an end at that very moment. A dark cloud came over her and for once, she didn't feel as though her life had any meaning or value to it.

"How could this be my reality of all people? There were dozens of girls who started having sex years before me and they aren't pregnant. I'm talking girls with no type of contraceptive at all. Those same girls bragged about no longer being virgins and now they're at the most popular HBCU living it up. Derrick was always careful when we were intimate. So I thought. For Pete's sake, we haven't even been intimate six full months yet. He is my first everything. Just in January losing my virginity was nearly a thought. I can't possibly have a baby growing in me. What in the world will my grandmother say? How will my uncle react? My younger cousins and sisters will never look up to me again. Why should they? I'm a failure. I'm never stepping foot in my home church again. The Boys & Girls

Club gave me a scholarship for college and now I'm carrying a child. A freaking CHILD. I'm still a baby myself that loves to sleep with her mother. Maybe she has the wrong room. I'm going to ask her to double-check her records. She was wrong. VERY WRONG."

"I'm afraid not," the doctor responded. "I would be glad to tell your mother if you don't have the confidence to do so. I understand this may not be the best news that you expected today."

Ummmm, clearly not, Sydney thought. The flu or food poisoning would have been a much easier pill to swallow. In fact, Sydney would probably pay for the doctor to switch the charts, out of her most recent financial aid payment. Sadly, this was not a joke or the latest game. This was reality. After doing what grown-ups do, it was time to pay the price.

The doctor invited Sydney's mom in the room and all she could do was stare at the floor with wells of water forming in the bottom of her eyelids. Making eye contact with her was nearly impossible at this moment. Her mom took the news much better than she ever would imagine. "I'm calling Derrick," were the next words that exited her mother's mouth. It took a few rings for him to answer but he finally did. "Sydney is pregnant," her mom told Derrick before he could even get a hello out.

Silence. Pure silence was all that came from Derrick's end of the receiver. You couldn't even hear him breathe. Later, her mom told her it was as if someone pressed "mute" on Derrick's cell phone without him knowing so. Sydney didn't ask to speak with him once her mother concluded the conversation. This news compared to a well-done steak and she hadn't digested it just yet. Truth is, she probably wouldn't any time soon.

Sydney, Derrick, and each of their mothers had a sit down as far as the next steps now that life for them would never be the same again. Her mother was adamant about Sydney finishing school and agreed to care for the baby until she completed her degree. Since Derrick was still in town and working full time, he could also be there to help both physically and financially. Sydney didn't have much to say days following the news they received. Thoughts of defeat and failure flooded her mind with no let up. If anything, she was concerned with what others would think and say of her, especially her grandmother and uncle. She never wanted to let them down and this news was sure to do that plus more.

The very short trip home resulting in life changing news had come to an end and it was time for her mother and Derrick to get her back up the road to Clark Atlanta. In a very small backseat, Sydney slept in Derrick's arms the entire four-hour car ride. They headed to the nearest Walmart for groceries just before checking back in at her dormitory. Sydney didn't want either of them to leave and made that quite clear through her whining just before watching her car navigate through the cul-de-sac to leave.

The next few days were interesting to say the least. Sydney woke up to a call from Derrick as she did any other day. He was her alarm clock and they always talked on his way to work. Following the call, she showered and prepared to tackle her day of classes. Little did she know, it would tackle her first. While walking to class under heat that seemed unbearable for it only to be nine in the morning, Sydney found tears rolling down her face uncontrollably. Whether this was hormones or emotions, she couldn't do it. She looked around at the smiles of others whom she did not know and couldn't let go of the fact that their entire world was before them and hers was about to end.

She turned back before even making it to the building and went to her room and planted her face in her pillows. Her life was over. "I can't do this," were the words she texted her mother and Derrick when she finally got enough strength to get out of the bed. A few hours later, her roommate walked in to Sydney on her knees vomiting wildly. She immediately grabbed a cold towel and tried to help her new "friend". Sadly, this was her new normal and Sydney made up her mind that she could not return to school. Over the next few days she took selfies of herself to prove to her mother she wasn't delusional but this pregnancy couldn't stand a chance if she stayed in her dorm four hours away with no proper nutrition or familiarity. Her great aunt and uncle lived approximately an hour away but Sydney couldn't imagine asking them to break their normal and come over to check on her daily. After a lot of convincing, her mother finally made up in her mind to rent an SUV and come to move Sydney back home.

Though back in her comfort zone, Sydney still had a tough time dealing with a baby growing inside of her. During her first trimester she lost thirty-two pounds and was hospitalized half a dozen times due to hyperemesis. Her grandmother prepared her most favorite meals and by the time it was ready, her appetite no longer desired it. Ironically, Sydney had no desire to be involved with Derrick physically or emotionally. The guy she once craved to be around, she could no longer stand to be in his space or he in hers. This was surely the case of hormones creeping in that Derrick never quite understood. In her mind, he ruined her future although it took both parties participating in the engagement of fornication. She trusted that he would make sure getting pregnant wasn't an option being as though he had a little more control. And now, all trust was lost, as she felt betrayed.

His mother tried to assure him that everything Sydney was going through was hormonal and would eventually fade away. It was common for women to not "like" their child's father while pregnant. Fortunately, Derrick wasn't willing to wait around for Sydney's moods and emotions to revert back to the pre-pregnancy days. He did what most men do and moved on. Sexually, that is. She was home watching soap operas daily while dry heaving, and he was already in another woman's face and shortly thereafter, her bed. Sydney's mother was nice enough to inform him of any doctor's visits and he never missed a single one. It was always awkward silence in the room but he made sure to be there. They both wanted a girl and once the ultra sound revealed just that, Derrick couldn't have been more excited.

One day out of the blue, Sydney woke up wanting to be in his arms again. It was weird. She texted him as soon as she could make it to the couch and told him she missed him. He was of course excited. A few days later and he was back to the normal routine of coming over every day after work. Sydney eventually became a little excited about the arrival of their little girl. She even went back to being the loving and caring girlfriend she was before the shocking news of them expecting a child together. Derrick was in need of a new cell phone so she made plans to gift him with a new phone for Christmas. A few months after receiving his gift, Sydney noticed he had a habit of texting every evening when he came over. The hormones and mood swings of disliking him had faded tremendously but Sydney couldn't help but begin to wonder who in the world he could be texting every single time he was over. His "boys" couldn't have that much to say. Watching *Snapped* probably didn't help thoughts of him cheating either. But as they say, a woman always knows. Her intuition typically never fails her.

Derrick had a tendency to doze off after a few hours of watching TV. Sydney couldn't help but do what any other girl who loved the man she would soon be welcoming a child with. She grabbed his phone and immediately began going through text messages. It appeared that Derrick was messaging someone daily, and telling them he was going to the gym at the same time he came to visit her every evening. Apparently this was someone he talked to every day and from the looks of it, she was a female. Sydney played it off and silently waited for Derrick to awake from his mini nap. Dozens of thoughts raced through her head, as this was the only man she had ever been intimate with. He had her heart and she couldn't imagine the possibility of him dipping out on her. Not now. Especially giving the circumstances and the season in which they were in.

Half an hour later Derrick began fidgeting, so she knew he would be leaving fairly shortly to get home and rest for work the following morning. She never uttered a word. Sydney walked him to the front door, gave him a kiss, and waited for him to kiss her belly as usual. She held back the tears like a professional actress. The moment she could no longer see his car from her window, she grabbed her phone and dialed the number she had memorized from Derrick's text messages.

A woman answered the phone. Silence. Sydney gathered her emotions and finally introduced herself. The woman on the other end knew exactly who she was. She knew Derrick had a child on the way but according to her, he was not with the mother of the unborn baby. Sydney cut right to the chase and asked the woman had she slept with Derrick. The female had no problem telling her with confidence, "yes, we slept together last week actually."

Click. She immediately fell to the ground, weeping uncontrollably. Her heart hurt. Sobs and screams woke her mother who came expeditiously in fear that she was going into labor. She wasted no time calling Derrick's mother to inform her of what just took place. Sydney could barely get out, with words, the news she had just received. Devastated. Empty. Betrayed. This felt like death. Her due date was just seven days away. How could he do this to her, while carrying their first baby? That night she cried, tossed and turned. The weight of the world felt as though it was dropped on her heart like the ball in Times Square on New Year's Eve night.

Two days later than her delivery date, Sydney began having contractions in the middle of the night. Her mom called Derrick's mother and told them to stay put just in case it was false labor. As soon as Sydney and her mother could make it back to triage to confirm the labor was active, Derrick and his mother arrived at the hospital. Her mother took a step out and allowed Derrick to come in. Two seconds in the room and Sydney immediately began yelling, "Why, why, why? Why, Derrick?"

He had no words. No words at all. The baby must have sensed her mother's upset spirit and started to do what looked like somersaults in her belly. This was going to be a long labor. The room was tense. Both sides of the families knew the events, which took place just a week prior. Fourteen long hours later and their baby girl entered the world. Friends and other family members came to meet her. They were parents and it was so surreal.

Sydney's sister wanted to stay the night at the hospital but they needed alone time. Some called it bonding time with their new baby. But deep down, Sydney still had questions and she was certainly going to get them out. Even if he was genuinely sorry, it didn't quite register. In fact, the female he slept with sent several text messages asking for pictures of his new baby. The nerve.

Over the next few years, things were pretty decent. Sydney slowly left God to accommodate Derrick merely based on what she assumed every man had to have in order for him to stay. Time and time again. As if she wasn't privy to the fact that God was a jealous God and would never come second to anyone. Not even a boy who possessed the "her first" title. She forsook her devotion and commitment to God for temporary romance. Poor romance at that. Romance that wanted her when it was convenient or when the other chick wasn't stroking his ego. She knew sex before marriage was not a part of God's will for His baby girl. She cheered herself on in her mind regularly in hopes that she could refrain from giving of herself to Derrick. She failed. Miserably.

Shortly after, Sydney and Derrick went as far as getting engaged. She wanted a real family. She wanted to do it right. She wanted to be his wife even after the pain she experienced with him. But this wasn't God's will. Needless to say, he moved on to other women while she waited for God's best. In spite of it all, Sydney refused to have different men in and out of her daughter's life. She was her first example and made a vow to herself that she would always be a good role model. Derrick dated several other women of a different race after they called it quits. He moved on to various women as though their love never amounted to much. It hurt Sydney deeply.

Several times she locked herself in the closet and just cried. She lost weight after a loss of appetite. It was hard to keep much down when her world seemed to be upside down. She tried to make it work when they were on good terms. Strategizing passcodes like a million-dollar prize was on the line became her normal. "Why did no one ever tell me the true value of my self-worth? Better yet, why didn't I listen?" She wondered. In the end, she was saving him while he was killing her.

With milk flowing from her breasts and shower water running down her back, tears dropped like an unexpected rainy day at the thought of ending things once again. The one he loved and respected the least loved and cherished him the most. My God did she want more for him than he could ever want for himself. Moving is said to be one of the third most stressful life events. No wonder moving on and finding herself was so hard. For a while, in her mind, he would never love another like he loved her.

Expectedly, after every failed relationship, he came back and asked for his family. They always said if you love something let it go, and if it comes back it was meant to be. NOT.

Could it be that it left because it was never designed to stay in the first place? Naïve at first, she took him back a few times. For some strange reason she thought this was real love. The fact that he could date other women and become intimate with them but still come back to her. She mistakenly thought this is what "special" felt like. At that point, she had no idea that love didn't hurt. Love was honest; it was pure, it was forgiving, and most importantly, love endured all. She stayed because she never wanted to ruin the one chance her daughter had growing up in a two-parent home that she missed out on. She broke the rules for him. It was the same rules she carved in her mind, vowing to never break for a single soul. Her main goal for her children was to never have to ask, "Whose weekend is it? Yours or dads?"

The years went on and Sydney focused more on self-development and strength concerning her relationship with God. He shut the door that she was never willing, nor had the courage or strength to close herself. But severing the connection was best for her and their daughter. That ending was the best beginning. His fatherhood traits worsened, as their daughter grew older. As they worsened, Sydney's bitterness grew greater. It was a little easier coming to terms with them not being a good match. Fortunately, God would never let what was lost be the best she ever had. Sometimes God has to break your heart in order to blow your mind. And she knew, embracing her future while having arms around her past was impossible.

Sydney deserved more and would not lower her standards only to accommodate the man she lost her virginity to. What she could not take was starting out very active in their daughter's life and that changing as different women came in and out of his life. Her frustration only increased and they arrived at a place where they couldn't have a cordial conversation with one another. So, it was best to not talk at all, even for the sake of their daughter. In a million years, Sydney never expected her first time experience as a mother to go this way. That grieved her badly. "How did I get here?" She wondered often. But only time would reveal the reason for such a stormy season. The sun would surely shine some day and God would make her laugh again.

Checking the child support website each morning became a normal routine just as washing her face and ironing clothes. "Extra funds" to do things she used to do prior to being a mom were far and few in between. Her daughter was her first priority always and anything for "self" was just not important. She became that mom, like most moms, who felt guilty any moment they even thought of purchasing something for themselves. While many assumed Derrick was a good father based on the image he portrayed on social media, the past due support owed grew more and more each month. That number always formed a sour taste in her mouth just glancing at it.

Hatred grew in her heart towards his employer as though she knew him personally. If there were a section dedicated for protestors against the child support enforcement agency, she'd skip work just to be there no matter what the consequences were. How could any employer not be concerned with the needs of his employee's children? After-school care, hair appointments, co-pay of doctor visits, and field trip funds all became her responsibility solely. Not to mention her weekly grocery bill since her daughter's school didn't have a cafeteria or offer lunch. His inability to provide for a child he helped create contributed to the distance between her and healing.

Occasionally, he made a visit to the school with cupcakes on her birthday, which left his social media in a frenzy believing he was this all-American dad. A wet pillow became the norm night after night as she cried herself to sleep in search of answers as to how someone could have offspring and not care to be involved concerning their well-being and day-to-day activities. In the beginning, Sydney's grandmother praised Derrick for being a good father. Honestly, any father who was a part of the child's life in some fashion was viewed as a great father mainly because the African American community was used to deadbeat fathers. Somehow social media displayed the complete opposite, causing others to believe she was telling lies or marked her as the "baby mama" who was only bitter because the two of them weren't together.

She didn't want him. Any of him. Even after the numerous times he came back after every single girlfriend. Of course many fathers aren't as hands on as mothers are, but there was clearly room for improvement on his behalf. Something as simple as checking to see how her school day went, afterschool enjoyment, or what upcoming ministry activities she was involved in at church was clearly asking for too much. Sydney yearned for the day she could see his love for their daughter in his eyes. She envied the relationship of fathers and daughters who made a place on her social media feed without invitation. Fathers who happened to be the same age as Derrick who would go to the moon and back just to see a smile on their daughter's face. Fathers who knew their daughter's or son's shoe size and didn't have to ask the child's mother. Fathers who showed up to parent-teacher conference or surprised their daughter with chocolate, flowers, and teddy bears on Valentine's Day as well as "just because" days. There were fathers who did NOT play about their daughters, and Sydney absolutely adored them. Let's not forget the fathers who would gladly show you their pistol if you even looked at their child with eyes, reflecting lustful desires for their princess.

Granny encouraged her periodically to pray for Derrick. Sydney didn't feel he was worthy so she never got around to penciling that on her prayer board. What she would do was pray that nothing good happened for him until he stepped up to be a better father. Not some every other weekend or once a month type father either. Nope. A one hundred percent committed father who doesn't wait for his child to call or acknowledge his position in her life. A father who stays connected to her teachers more than she did. A father who makes plans for father/daughter time and lets nothing interrupt or interfere with those obligations, not even the most gorgeous woman on her bad day. A father who doesn't believe in child support because no judge or system can equate his responsibilities of providing for her in many ways. Now that, God; that's something she would pray for.

She was certainly not the most obedient child of all her siblings. Sydney was a little rebellious and rough around the edges from time to time. Though she prayed and asked for complete healing, God's assignments should have been identified as extra credit for this was surely not on the syllabus when she registered for the course. Over the years she'd read about difficult tasks God asked others to do. And although it looked impossible or rather irrational, the task was completed. She remembered God telling Peter to walk on water, Noah to build an ark, and Abraham to sacrifice his only son. In every situation, it didn't make sense. Praying for her child's father was surely to be added to an amended version of the Bible.

January 13, 2016 was a night she didn't need to mark on her calendar, as she was sure to remember it forever. God nudged her gently to wake up in the middle of the night, just three hours shy of her alarm going off for another busy day of work and tending to her daughter. For the last six months she ignored these wake up calls. She felt like God knew she needed rest and that she could always pray and converse with Him on her thirty to forty-five minute treacherous commute each morning. Her praying mentor brought to her attention that though she needed rest, she always managed to get the many other things done Sydney wished to do. So, this night in particular, she forced herself to be obedient to His spirit and arise.

The smell of her morning, or should we say middle of the night breath, and crust in her eyes, didn't matter. She flipped the cover and got up. And just like that, He began to speak. She grabbed her phone, prepared to write what thus said the Lord. To get her in the right mood and set the tone of the atmosphere, she quickly opened her YouTube app and chose a worship song she'd had on replay for the last three days. "Alright big guy, I'm ready when you are. I'm sure You know this bed has me hostage with sleep I so honestly need before my work day begins."

Moments later she'd almost wished He never beckoned for her to awake. God began to speak. But just a few short moments later, He asked her to do "it" again. Yes, "it". Why must He continue to ask me to do what simply isn't beneficial for me or my daughter for that matter? Sydney thought. "You want healing, pray for him." Come on, God, not today. Please let me just get back to bed and we can both forget this "divine intervention" ever happened. Deal? For once, Sydney experienced silence from God. It was a silence that definitely scared her for a moment. He went from speaking to complete silence. Never did she wish to make Him angry or cause His spirit to grieve in disappointment. On the other end, by no means was God interested in negotiating a deal with her. Besides, He was her father and not the other way around. This was simply not a part of His nature.

She sat for a few moments. The softened worship music had now been put on pause. For what God was preparing for her life, she knew then more than ever, obedience was better than sacrifice. The sleep she could always make up for, but any download from Heaven was worth it. In all honesty, she wanted to be an obedient little girl. One that had her Father wrapped around her little fingers. But also, one who stayed in a child's place as the seasoned folk said, and listened with intent of following specific instructions. She was no "baby" in Christ, so submission to direction and assignments was far from foreign territory.

Sydney sat there a little longer. The suede comforter had now made its way between her recently shaved legs as she debated going back to sleep. She took a deep breath and squeezed her eyes tightly hoping this was just a bad dream that would be over momentarily. She opened one eye to look around, making sure what she saw was familiar. By this time, she figured she would take a quick break for a glass of green tea as if she needed a break for something she hadn't been doing just yet. The thought of praying for someone she felt so underserving made her mouth dry before she could even gather her thoughts.

"Fathe..." She tried to utter the first few words to begin what would probably be the shortest prayer of her life. Even shorter than her child's grace over dinner but ehhh, who's timing right? It was almost like the enemy stood there from behind with a tight grip around her neck, preventing a single word from escaping. "I can do this, I can do this," she told herself repeatedly. "Father in the na…" This time, the oppressor had an even tighter grip around her neck. It was almost as though he was pissed that she was even trying to do such things. If the night-light were on, she may have witnessed the marks from his holding, which became more unbearable. It was as though he threatened her life if she even as much as thought God would use her in any capacity. It was actually no coincidence that this was taking place.

Strangely enough, God had given Sydney a new revelation a few weeks ago, which further confirmed her purpose in the Earth realm. Women of all backgrounds and walks of life would begin gathering in a windy line behind Sydney as she traveled from state to state. Just as the line leader in grade school, until the head gets in line, others wouldn't know how to get in formation. The line would grow longer and longer as she approached each state. In essence, she was destined to lead masses of women if she could only get over herself.

Daily, this became a habit just as her normal schedule was. Before she realized, the wound was slowly but surely getting smaller and smaller. He had to step in and rescue her when she felt unworthy of being saved. He had to bring her to a place of full repentance after realizing she was stinking in a funky place. God was healing her. Yes, healing. There was nothing she could do to stop what He was transforming in her life, even if she wanted to. She allowed the usage of her lips to thank Him frequently. Worthy He was.

***

A love letter to my uterus,

If I could only turn back the hands of times, oh how different things would have been. Allowing a man to enter your most sacred place who hadn't even earned a hello would have never been a tiny thought on my most bored day. I used you before I ever knew your value. A price tag doesn't have the capacity to hold all that you carry. Apologizing probably isn't worth it, but I can't go on without sincerely asking for your forgiveness. Though it's so easy to play the victim and ask why no one ever warned me of your power, I'll walk in maturity and accept the customizable consequences of my actions and poor misjudgment.

Forgiveness may not be on your radar at this very moment and I can accept that. But rose, since everything is out there now, there is one little thing I would like to admit. That's if it's okay with you. Though I violated the potency of your existence, I can say that if the chance presented itself again, I would take it. Before you decide to stop reading out of anger and disbelief, and ball this letter up maybe, hear me out for a second. What I took from you forced me to grow up in ways I probably never would have yielded to had this not been the case. And I'm not talking about a few inches. This experience has been the catapult to a destiny hand-picked by God to free millions.

What I'm trying to say is despite robbing you of something money could never buy, you gave me a gift that could never be wrapped perfectly, because it in itself is perfect. You gave me a new set of eyes that couldn't possibly need a prescription. You gave me closeness with our Father that I never had the guts to ask for because I never knew I needed it. You gave me a new life full of big dreams and hopes that continue to require big faith to receive. In essence, you gave me ME. The un-pretty me. The unfiltered me that radiates beauty on its worst day. The "me" behind many masks crying for an escape. Rather than kill me softly, you found a way to love me gently. My God, you have no idea how much you mean to me.

Sincerely,
Your biggest fan

Expired

I will make you into a great nation, and I will bless you; I will make your name great, and you will be a blessing. (Genesis 12:2) (NIV)

And I am certain that God, who began the good work within you, will continue his work until it is finally finished on the day when Christ Jesus returns. (Philippians 1:6)(NLT)

Before I formed you in the womb I knew you, before you were born I set you apart; I appointed you as a prophet to the nations. (Jeremiah 1:5)(NIV)

Pinned papers. Sticky notes. Black crates carrying useless papers. Bent chords and wires stretched behind HP monitors. A confined space. Like a cell without the bars. Her name was "cubicle." Five days a week. Eight-hour days. Horrible commutes. Numerous wrecks and the aftermath witnessed. Thousands of added mileage yearly. Prostituted gifts and talents. Serving millionaires. Bank account on empty. Updating beneficiaries wondering how my own children would ever inherit wealth. Story of my life.

I don't belong here.

My counterparts don't look the way I do. For them,

this is success. For me, this is defeat. This is failure to have a calling, gifts, talents, and second to none work ethic and be caged in day by day. My gifts didn't need to be stirred or ignited by any means. I was a firecracker all by myself. No pep rally or motivational YouTube video was ever needed to get my adrenaline going. I was and always will be a self-starter. If only I could self-start this thing called destiny.

The Lord has need of me. Why am I here? The cubicle had been a place of prison for the last eight years and it was past time for a new normal. How could I affluence and influence the masses with three walls surrounding me daily? The eagle had stirred the nest and I believed it was past time for me to be free and soar like the eagle God called and created me to be. So I thought. The kind of liberty of waking up, knowing I only had to answer to my purpose that day is all I desire. If and when God says "go," I can go with no restrictions. Is that too much to ask for?

The land was mine and I had contended for it over several years. I had sown seed after seed that should have granted a harvest by now that would cause me to be in my fruitful place. A place of deliverance from micromanagement. A place where I could be free and operate in that which sets my soul on fire. The soil was good and so was the seed. Again, so I thought. Yet here I was in a holding pattern. Awaiting permission to land. Permission from whom, you ask? God. It was definitely a state of inaction with no progress and no change. Day after day. Talk about merely existing.

Hour lunches and fifteen minute breaks started out as heaven and slowly matured to a death sentence. Perhaps you've seen the quote by Ellen Goodman that states, "Normal is getting dressed in clothes that you buy for work, driving through traffic in a car that you are still paying for, in order to get to a job that you need so you can pay for the clothes, car, and the house that you leave empty all day in order to afford to live in it." I don't really like that normal anymore. Not to be taken sarcastically at all. A few years ago this was certainly my dream job. You know, the one you tell everyone about with a sigh of relief you'd finally managed to find your career and you're no longer settling for just a "job". Getting here was far from a walk in the park.

My employer took pride in hiring the cream of the crop and as I mentioned my counterparts and colleagues don't look quite the way I do. Favor brought me here.

Initially, I carried the excitement as any employee would once they finally joined a decent company. Initially, I marked this place as my final destination before retirement. So I thought. Everyone looked extremely professional and the chef made such delicious meals daily. I mean, what else could a girl ask for? Freedom, that's what.

It didn't take long to realize my skin color wasn't the only thing that set me apart or forced me to feel out of place. I could imagine my colleagues were probably raised in two-parent homes with parents who had great careers and a lofty 401k or pension plan. Parents who pushed them to be all they could be and made provisions for their children to be well-rounded throughout their childhood. Parents who could afford for their precious babies to attend the best private schools while gathering top-notch education. Parents who never had to witness a financial aid application because little Sarah and Graham had money set aside probably prior to even being born by their parents and grandparents.

I know. Because I've talked to parents like them and saw checks scanned in while working in our processing departments directly from grandparents investing anywhere from ten dollars bi-weekly to one hundred dollars a month for their legacy. Maybe it was then, processing those checks that began the seed planting of wanting even more for my own life and descendants. God had called me to be a rule breaker, legacy breaker, generational curse breaker, planet shaker, trendsetter, and much more. His ways and thoughts have always been higher than my own. I found it interesting when I applied for a permanent position at my employer the second go-round that I closed out the final position in our department that catered to millionaires specifically. Yep, you read that right. Out of all applicants there happened to be ONE position left in the department that is tailored to cater to clients with at least one million dollars in net assets.

I'm certain you've realized now this certainly wasn't by happenstance, but more of a divine orchestration from my father, God. Not to stop there, the two managers I happened to interview with raved about my experience to my manager and others until it got back to me. It's funny how God works sometimes. Maybe, just maybe, He desired for me to converse with millionaires daily so once He placed me in the presence of these type of individuals, I would know how to carry myself with dignity and much confidence. He's such a thoughtful God. Training was long.

Very long. I was ready for my new role after days and weeks of countless training that honestly wasn't beneficial to the job at hand. The first few months were exciting and stressful all in one. Eventually, the career I couldn't wait to obtain was pushed to the "job" pile just like previous roles.

Don't get me wrong; the company is certainly one of the best. But now, I understand that only certain types of individuals should be employed with them. Employees. And that doesn't fit who I am any longer. There are people who were born to lead, which mean there are those who were born to simply follow. I am not the latter. Micromanagement wasn't a major deal like with most companies. For me, it was the knowing that I served a higher purpose on this here Earth. And the cubicle didn't have the ability to allow me to thrive in that arena. Again, a holding cell. I found myself doing just enough to stay employed but not enough to get promoted. I made sure to not stand out with my performance just in case they deemed it a good idea for me to train anyone new to the department. Sound familiar? I worked on personal goals in between calls to take advantage of every minute spent here.

Setting a Monday through Friday alarm clock, knowing I wasn't awaking to fulfill my destiny was torture.

My generation and countless others have been mentally programmed to work forty hour weeks for forty years building another man's dream to only pray for enough savings to retire by the age of sixty-five. In my eyes, this happened to be the definition of settling, and I couldn't accept it. My spirit yearned to be in the presence of other believers who were determined to make their dreams a reality, no matter the expense. Individuals who thought outside the box and didn't mind exchanging sweat and tears if it meant setting the stage for the descendants and building a strong legacy. Unlike my peers, I never desired to be a millionaire overnight. A strong work ethic was never an issue for me being as though my mother worked twelve to fourteen-hour days to ensure that my sister and I had what children in two-parent homes had. I didn't mind putting in the work if it meant laying the foundation for a fresh start without debt for my heirs.

What I wasn't for was working a job, eight hours a day, sitting through traffic and coming home uninspired to work and build on my own empire. Not on my watch. In fact, my best work was done on the company's watch. For some odd reason, while sitting in that cubicle, I gathered the most inspiration to put the pen to the paper and pursue my goals even the more. Daily I challenged myself to not leave the "plantation" without a certain amount of words written. And now, you're reading the pages of my novel. It's amazing what happens when a determined woman refuses to settle.

But back to my frustration. As we know, social media has the power of allowing us to see the daily lives of many. It's now a commonality for many to post aspects of their occupation or how their time is allotted throughout the day. The same for those self-employed as well. And of course, those who were walking in their calling and destiny seemed to show more than frequently on each of my social media platforms. I scrolled through daily, envying those who weren't subject to a supervisor or cubicle, and those who made their own schedules who actually weren't hairdressers. Those who could travel at the drop of a dime or eat lunch with their children when they felt like doing so as opposed to asking for permission from their bosses. Those who could take a trip to the mall in the middle of the afternoon on a Tuesday. And let's not even talk about those whose commute to their "job" were merely a few steps from their bedroom to their office. Inserts side eye followed by an eye roll.

It's never been about a hefty salary or bank account for me. It's been about walking freely in my calling to reach those connected to me by assignment without asking for time off or worrying about how many hours were left in the PTO bank. It was about going to volunteer at my child's school on any given day or sitting through the pickup line for close to an hour just to see the huge smile that stretched from ear to ear when she realized her mother was picking her up and not the afterschool program's twelve-seat passenger van. Freedom is not to be enjoyed only on the weekends. Sunday nights soon became 'come to Jesus' meetings as I had to prepare for another workweek of taking instructions from millionaires when I should have been spending time working to gain my millions. It wasn't enough to have "potential" to be a millionaire. That word actually became a word that when heard, I felt a negative connotation associated with it.

I never want to be remembered by the girl who had much "potential". No. She was the girl who went and got whatever it was God had for her with no reservations. He had more, and I've been made aware of this for years now. Nothing is allowed to be left on the table. If it's for me, trust that I'm going to get it all. It has never helped that I'm the girl amongst my friends with the old soul. I am woman. What does that mean? It means that I have the power to take the seed of an idea and turn it into an amazing event. Women are said to be incubators of dreams. We can take the seed of a conversation or thought and turn it into a best-selling novel. Checkmate. Still young, but in my mind, I'm much older which means I don't have time to play around and slack with complacency and mediocrity.

Let's talk about time for a minute. Perhaps this has been my biggest challenge mentally. Living and thinking in terms of chronos and not Kairos. There is a difference. Chronos typically refers to chronological or sequential time that's quantitative. All of our lives we are taught the significance of time as it relates to minutes, hours, days, and so forth, that have framed our mindset. We define seasons by time. We have a list of things to do according to time. We have deadlines according to time and even set goals with specific timeframes to achieve them. Yes, scripture tells us to number our days and we know that our time on earth is very brief. Ironically, the chronos mindset tends to make us miss the importance of seasons as it relates to our destiny and predestined end. Most of my life, up until recently, I've always lived based on an internal time clock. I wanted to buy a home by age twenty-five and get married by this time, and have children by that time. I'm sure you're nodding in agreement now.

Though God puts different desires in our hearts, it doesn't mean that we are left to dictate when they occur and deviate from the set time that He desires to give us those things. There is a season and time for everything. That's biblical. If in every season my eyes are always fixed on the next, how can I enjoy the current state that I'm in? I can also attest to the fact that I wasn't always in a place of maturity and faith to even receive such blessings. When things didn't happen the minute I thought they should, based on a deadline I created myself, I characterized that season as a sad season of waiting. I ushered myself into a place of unbelief while leaving God with the task of restoring a lost hope. God knew and still knows so much more than I can see with my natural eyes. What I didn't realize before was the fact that I serve the author of time who could get me "there" overnight if He wanted to. Literally. I've prayed, "Order my steps, Lord," all while trying to do so myself. Looking in hindsight, it means the world to have a father who loves me enough not to give me something ahead of maturity just to satisfy my impatience.

Let's take a look at Kairos. This view suggests some moments are more valuable than others. It gives the confidence that though I live in a world where everything is based on time, there is also another "time" that has the power to remove the anxiety of "when" and prepare my heart and mind knowing that it's not a question as to "if" it will occur. The mere fact that God said it "would" happen takes the need away to debate or question His word. My deepest fear has always been dying without living first. No, that absolutely can't be my story. When I go on to glory, I plan to be completely empty, for I used and poured out everything to everyone during my time on this side of heaven. When God created us, it was with the intention of us being fruitful, multiplying, and having dominion on Earth. He never designed us to live in a box and walk around with a limited level of thinking. Absolutely not.

I would gather that He finds pleasure and joy witnessing His children live out loud and bask in His will for their lives. Handouts are not and never will be a part of the mind of individuals desiring success with the proper mindset and work ethic. It's not enough to have hundreds of magazines, markers, stationary, and positive affirmation notes to create the most creative dream and vision boards if we never put our hands to the plow and put in the work. More often than not, we lack accountability and discipline. We have wonderful ideas and will actually jump-start those ideas long enough to get a little buzz. As soon as things go astray or we feel as though life is too hard or it's not possible to see it through to the end, we give up. Sadly, this wasn't my issue. I had a deeper problem. And it was deep rooted.

God has kept me hidden for a reason I never quite understood. Every vision, dream, download from heaven, and countless other confirmations never added up to where I was currently. For the life of me I couldn't figure out why I seemed to be in such a "stuck" manner if you will. And then it was revealed. Bitterness didn't affect only my relationships with God, others, and myself. It also had the power to affect my success in my career. Wow. When I thought I could control the perimeters to which "it" was confined to, it bled to every other area of my life. Other areas I had blocked off with numerous signs that were visible to "it's" eye. Now wait a minute. This thing had gone too far and overstepped way too many boundaries. I had a choice. I could continue "playing" dumb and crying out to God for answers as to why I didn't seem to be progressing. Or, I could woman up and confront "it". I'm talking about the confronting when other kids at school have been bullying your babies and talking with the principal or child's teacher was out of the question. The confronting you probably did in high school when you found out another chick had been bad mouthing you or talking to your guy behind your back. Oh, yeah. It was serious at this point.

I had countless revelations as it relates to my future and the plans He has for me. Those revelations never stood alone. I also had stubborn faith to see it without "seeing" it. But that mustard seed of faith was thrown out the window and deemed null and void when bitterness stepped on the scene. She was wide and big enough to not let a single thing behind that fruitful place behind her. Did I mention she was serious about protecting what she thought was "her" territory? She never slept or took a nap. I compare her to the enemy that roars around like a lion, seeking whom he may devour. It's safe to say she peeked back there a time or two and knew what I was forfeiting with my refusal to lay aside that thing that so easily besets me.

Maybe you too have found yourself in a place where everything you try just isn't working. What if your work ethic wasn't the issue? Perhaps you too are extremely talented, creative, self-motivated and driven but yet can't escape the conditions and restrictions of your now. What if your current state has nothing to do with geography and all to do with an inward blood clot formed by an enemy determined to produce your demise? I am far from perfect. Believe me. But I decided I could not stomach taking a front row seat and watch "it" expand territory with land of mine that I gave over with no fight. What will you choose today?

A Couple of Whenevers

And so it was....that she, having waited long & endured patiently realized and obtained what God had promised. (Hebrews 6:15)(AMP)

Wait on the Lord; be of good courage, and He will strengthen your heart; wait, I say, on the Lord. (Psalm 27:14)(KJV)

You can hold on to the hope that I will not change what I have promised. (Hebrews 6:17-18)

"What in the world is wrong with you, Nita?"

"Not now, mama."

"I'm not one of your little friends and I'm certainly not going to beg you. Tell me NOW, Nita Marie!"

"If I see one more surprise proposal, gender reveal party video, or another picture of a home closing, I'm going to LOSE it. Seriously considering deleting my social media pages. I can't scroll through my newsfeed without seeing something that reminds me of the promise that just refuses to manifest for whatever reason. I don't understand. I wake up each day waiting, to only wait again, and then wait some more. Just call me Ms. Wait for Pete's sake."

"Sweetheart, haven't we been through this before? Your happiness is not contingent on others. Celebrate with them, knowing your time will come. You know the old saying; if God is blessing your neighbor, He's headed to your house next, or at least in the neighborhood. I've told you a dozen times now to stop comparing your valley experience to their debut talk show. That's not healthy and it's definitely not godly. Has God spoken and it not came to pass? God said He has purposed and so will He do it. You doubt Him too much. You should stop that."

"MOM! No disrespect. But I do not need nor want your wisdom and faith in God thrown at me right now. I don't need you to be the fifty-year-old mom forcing yourself to give wisdom that grandmamma would give. Some washed up advice only so you can say to yourself later you said the right thing. NO, mom. I need you to go back into time and transform into your twenty-five-year-old self again. Just for a minute. Why are you being so insensitive? Don't you realize how many times I've been around this mountain? How many lessons am I to learn? How many tests until I finally pass this class? I need you to sympathize with my current love deficit. Do you realize the ratio of good men to women nowadays? I am almost positive for every good man there are about ten worthy women waiting to be found.

"What did I do wrong? I mean, my shape is decent. I've gotten good at sucking in certain areas when I'm not wearing my top-notch girdle. I can slay with a bangin' outfit and give a fierce makeup look on a good day with about two hours minimum locked in the bathroom with my favorite Pandora station blasting through my wireless speakers. My heart is pure and I even go to church faithfully. I just stepped up to be the vice president of the singles ministry. I'm finally consistently paying my tithes. You'd be happy to know that I sowed a thirty-one dollar seed recently when the guest Pastor persuaded singles to sow this specific seed if they believed God for a husband. It represents a Proverbs thirty-one woman. Clearly, He doesn't love me much if He continues to allow me to watch others get what He knows my heart desires.

"Do you realize how difficult it is to pray to a God who knows exactly what makes you smile without realizing and He's dangling that exact thing in your face and refuses to manifest it? Do you remember when Uncle David use to hold candy above his head and watch me jump up and down tirelessly as if I would ever reach it? I mean the dude was six foot five easily. Same unfortunate and most of all impossible scenario with God. Only this time I feel He's about ten feet tall and that's on a good day. I would love to know the why behind Him holding up this one tiny little thing. What is the point of even praying anymore? I see no signs of any changes with my natural eyes. I have read Psalm 84:11 so many times that now if I even see the scripture, I roll my eyes. The fact that "hope deferred makes the heart sick" is included in the Bible blows my mind."

As she continued speaking, she quickly lowered her voice and changed her tone after remembering this was the same woman who didn't mind grabbing a few "switches" from the nearest tree in the backyard and tearing her behind up regardless of age. That same woman would grab the nearest object and use it for her benefit at the drop of a dime. And she was heavy handed. Bad combination.

At the tender age of twenty-seven, Nita wasn't concerned with being intimate with a guy unlike other girls her age. Her world didn't revolve based on whether or not a man was present in her life. In fact, she was never one to give of her body with just any ol' boy. Oh, no, he certainly had to bring more than a nice physique to the table that she was more than capable of building herself. She had standards, and every guy in town knew that. Come correct or don't even bother with wasting her time. She wanted to fall in love, but not like social media showed "love". Absolutely not. I'm talking nineties R&B type love. That Usher and Brandy or even Que' from Moesha kind of love. Martin and Gina were a little more realistic. She was different. She saw life differently. She had visions that were merely uncommon for someone of her age and background. And my God was there a special call on her life. She had a special glow about her that was second to none. Something like a class all by herself. Building a legacy for herself and future descendants was always the goal. It was the number two goal behind God's will. She worked, as though rent was due daily and her future children had no option for financial aid for higher education.

Yes, a hustle like none other. No matter the consistent, unqualified, resilient boys who showed up in her social media inbox almost quarterly, she was focused. She was focused and determined to never settle, no matter how "enticing" the offering seemed. She dodged the few that supported her business like the best running back in history. Over the years, God showed her many things in the spirit. She had a vision that was so keen she could see even in the dark for miles. She found herself just waiting for them to manifest. There goes that "w" word again. Waiting, waiting, and more waiting. But one day, God was going to hold her up like a trophy for the world to see. He was going to show the universe, 'this is what happens when you trust in Me with all your heart and lean not into your own understanding.'

One day, while headed to work, three eagles flew in front of Nita's windshield for what she believed was intentional. Being the person who seeks revelation in all things, she immediately asked God what He was revealing and that she wouldn't stop asking until she received a concrete answer. Being the man He is, He answered by the time she made it to the work parking lot. He explained just as clear as day that the three eagles represented Nita, her husband, and child traveling the world, speaking. On her way home that evening, she saw planes taking off left and right. God concluded the revelation by explaining further that she and her future husband would travel from city-to-city, state-to-state, and country-to-country encouraging and inspiring the masses. In her mind, she would take a guy with a vision for his future and could lead a woman over a "boy" whose sole purpose in life was standing in line on a rainy, Saturday morning for the latest pair of Air Jordans.

Her top love languages were quality time and words of affirmation. She didn't need the latest Louboutin's or designer jeans. The hottest Brahmin bag couldn't put a dent on the type of affection that made her soul happy. She yearned for a man with short term as well as long term goals who enjoyed Mali Music concerts just as much as she did, could lift up holy hands and worship God in total adoration, and actually understand the importance of courtship before getting any of her cookies. That jar was sealed shut. And yes, a man who could court her. Somewhere along the way we gave up chivalry in exchange for a boy that could post a few "Woman Crush Wednesday" posts every now and then. A boy who was used to whispering sweet nothings, and who possessed no earthly or spiritual idea for leading a virtuous woman. For Nita, there was something about a man worshiping God that was a true turn-on. A man who could hold an intelligent conversation without using profanity or complimenting her curves in a disrespectful manner was always welcoming. How dare we forget a spontaneous man who could plan a date without asking his female cousins for assistance or using the Google search feature on his iPad?

Not even Pinterest. Road trips with Pandora on blast, singing their hearts out to the hottest slow jams from the eighties and nineties didn't seem too bad either.

Being single for the majority of her twenties was something she felt sad about some days, and other days she was proud of the woman she'd grown to become over the years. Besides, "they" say your twenties should be spent building and setting the stage for your thirties. She was definitely that type of gal. Quite frequently, the enemy had a sneaky way of making her feel as though her singleness was punishment, torture, and would only leave her old with two fat, ugly black cats before her forties came to a close. I mean clearly she had her own place so she never had to worry about privacy or her little sister busting in her room door "if" something inappropriate were to pop off. Granny was fifteen to twenty minutes away and her mother worked way too many hours to randomly pop up at her place. She repeatedly reminded God that she was free to do adult things even if conviction came afterwards. She wanted Him to know how hard refraining from any type of intimacy really was. Her prayer partner consistently brought to her attention the Apostle Paul's story in the Bible. Paul was absolutely crazy in saying that he had learned to be content in whatever state he was in. Hogwash indeed. And even if he was content, Nita was sure it was only for a season or he wasn't all man. Nita was the girl who'd planned her wedding in her head for years. Pinterest never made this obsession any easier. Color schemes, wedding venues, engagement photo ideas and locations, dresses for she and her most favorite girls, all the way down to the shock on her face the day of the proposal circled her mind without noticing on any giving day. Oh, and not to mention the famous hashtags depending on his last name. She couldn't hold a tune on her best day in the shower or in the car during five o' clock traffic, but she had a few songs up her sleeve she anticipated lip singing to her special guy on their big day.

Her guy. She liked the sound of that. A guy designed and fashioned just for her. His rib. With little to no rhythm, a special dance performance of "Cater to You" for her man was merely a thought. He would have to catch that behind closed doors. Way behind closed doors. Try the walk-in closet. The theme and season of her well planned-out wedding varied from time to time, considering God hadn't slid the right man in her DM or to her church as the armor bearer with a visiting pastor. Giggles. He honestly didn't even have to be the pastor's direct adjutant. Just ole faithful who traveled with him to minister the gospel from time to time. The numerous Facebook assessments did a good job of giving her hope from day to day. In fact, some tests she purposely did over and over until she got the current year as a result of the timeframe in which Boaz would come out of hiding or her Adam would wake up.

After a while, she forced herself to avoid certain Instagram and Facebook pages in order to prevent high hopes from being smashed again. The holidays never made it any easier. Oddly enough, the same posts and pages she chose to avoid somehow made it to her newsfeed or the popular page. The very love songs she'd added to the playlist for her reception mysteriously played on her gospel Pandora station almost daily. Who said God didn't have a sense of humor? Her former first lady told her specific-detailed prayers could certainly be made a reality. Though she didn't voice those desires aloud, she certainly shouted her must-haves in her head and even in her overly used journal. Oh, and her closest girlfriends knew "her type". The mother of the church also told her she had a vision of Nita walking down the aisle in a dress that was to die for. She went on to tell her one day she would come back and say, "Mother Grier told me it would be beautiful." Nita really appreciated the prophecies and visions from others. But at the same time, it was a little discouraging and hard to not keep track of the days, hours, and minutes which had gone by and no manifestation of a single thing yet. Not even a good guy friend she could phone or text when she wanted to have "love" talk. Eventually, Nita found herself in a place of pleading with God not to reveal any other pieces of the puzzle until He was ready to show her something she could see with her natural eyes. A tangible manifestation of His promises. The visions led to frustration and ultimately sadness.

One day, Nita came across a video that went viral on Facebook of a couple who waited on God's promises for years. Coincidentally, God had told both husband and wife they would one day be the parents of a daughter name Chloe. They waited four years and still no sign of a positive pregnancy test. It was a little embarrassing attending baby showers and first birthday parties for their closest friends all while doubting God and crying daily over what seemed to be a barren womb. They were forced to hide their deepest pain with smiles that hid watered eyelids. Eventually, the couple came to terms with the possibility of not being able to biologically parent a child. Inflexible, adoption was out of the picture for the husband. If God wasn't big enough to give them their own seed, they sure as heck didn't want a second-hand child. After some time, they took their minds off watering thoughts of being parents and lived life as they always had. Alone. Just the two of them.

Years, months, and days went by. The wife had become bitter with God and couldn't fathom why He'd put a desire in their hearts that wouldn't and couldn't be brought to fruition. With tears flowing without force, Nita loved the transparency the wife showed. It was real to question God's whereabouts and trust that He cares when there seems to be no sign or trace of Him present. Rather than pretend this fairytale faith existed, the wife spoke of her doubts and frustrations with God. Seeing someone so relatable gave Nita a few doses of hope. Shortly after taking their focus off being parents to this natural born daughter, the couple considered adoption. That's right. Even after the husband was completely against it. To take things further, they were even informed they would soon be adoptive parents of a baby girl. They met with the biological mother at her small home prior to her scheduled due date. When talking for what may have seemed like hours, the pregnant woman informed the highly anxious couple that she had been calling the baby "Chloe."

Immediately, tears began to flow from both the husband and wife. Oh, and Nita had literally cried a river at this point. Everything they endured seemed so minuscule at that very moment. It was already mind blowing that God had given both parents the name Chloe before they ever even met. The vision of the little girl in the husband's mind matched the first view of the tiny baby exactly. God never forgot His promises for this couple. Though it took years to manifest, IT DID. Nita was so excited for them. But she just needed a miracle to happen for HER.

Just when she planned to rock the idea of the perfect wedding and living happily ever after asleep, she received a text message from a high school friend asking to meet up the following weekend. With little hesitation, Nita agreed. Traffic was always ridiculously insane at the local Starbucks any day of the week. She was tempted to use the handicap parking space and grab her grandmother's placard from the glove compartment but digressed. A fine of any amount just wasn't feasible or welcoming for her tight budget. She threw her turning signal on to make sure the car coming down the opposite way knew the parking space, which seemed closer to them, was indeed hers. As she pulled "Midnight" in the parking space, she was greeted with a text message from her homegirl letting her know she was already inside seated.

Nita wasn't sure what this was about and surely didn't care for coffee but took a deep breath and headed inside. Perhaps they would have a good smoothie her friend could treat her to. Ashleigh knew Nita was on a new health journey since the New Year and was kind enough to have a fresh strawberry smoothie waiting for her as she had hoped. They greeted with a hug and sat down to discuss the purpose of their long overdue meeting. After much small talk and catching up on the latest local gossip, social media trends, and family rivalry, Ashleigh finally revealed her reasoning for such an impromptu mini date. She reached in her oversized bag to grab Nita a small cardboard box approximately the shape of a cubic square with "Will you?" written in a blue Sharpie on top. With squinted eyes and wrinkled forehead, Nita opened the box to find a red ring pop with the wrapper removed. "I would love for you to share my special day with me and be by my side as a bridesmaid," voiced Ashleigh with the biggest grin on her face. Never before had Nita realized how beautiful Ashleigh's pearly whites were since her braces were removed until that day. With no hesitation, Nita immediately responded, "Sure, I would love to."

She had a tendency of agreeing to things and then later coming to terms with what she had committed to. There's a good chance of a nice pillow talk going down once she got in and settled. A good cry may even be necessary once this decision is processed. Nita had certainly gotten good with holding back tears until she could release herself the way she so desperately needed to. Though cutting back on her Moscato intake was a part of her New Year's resolution, tonight called for an exception along with lighting her most recent Bath & Body Works candle. Honestly, wine may not even do the trick. She needed a "drank". Celebrating others even when they had what she desired was always top five on the prayer list for Nita. As tough as it was most days, she prayed that God would give her the strength to genuinely celebrate others so when her time came, others could do the same. Being bitter was one trait she tried to do away with for years. Not to mention fake happiness wasn't something she could hide very well. Scrolling through Facebook forcing herself to hit the like and sometimes even love button was all a part of the masking. And honestly, there was no point in faking it when God knew every single one of her thoughts anyway. This would actually be Nita first wedding in quite a while.

Years ago, she remembered being a flower girl for her grandparents' wedding but that really didn't count. This was two totally different experiences and sets of emotions altogether. At that moment, she'd actually prefer to be a little flower girl again rather than deal with the host of feelings that overcame her mind in that given moment. Maybe God would come through with a man of her own for a date, Nita thought. If not, this could possibly be the first time she considered some sort of escort service. According to recent reality TV shows, this was the thing to do in desperate measures. And she was sadly desperate. God had to know she didn't want to show up to the wedding with no one to slow dance with or get in front of for the well-anticipated Soul Train line. Nita was drained. Not physically, but emotionally. Grandmomma would remind her to be not weary in well doing. But Nita was at the stage after weariness at this point. More like miserable. She wrapped up the get-together with Ashleigh with a hug and kiss on the cheek as she turned to walk to her car with her head hung. Nita jumped in her Jeep and quickly shut her phone off. Not even Pandora could fix the broken pieces that shattered inwardly as she sat there without movement. She waited for what seemed like an eternity for Ashleigh to finally pull off.

As soon as she could see her tag at the light in her rearview mirror, Nita let the tears have their way. Thoughts of all kind flooded her mind without permission. Unqualified, unworthy, not enough, or too much were just a few adjectives that came to mind to describe her in her current state. The Bible and God's promises said one thing. Meanwhile, reality said the complete opposite. Unfortunately, reality won more times than she wished to admit. At that moment, Nita began to doubt her value and the God she'd placed all her hope in. To be honest, not being in control and giving someone full power over your destiny was a little difficult at times. Her great aunt loved to infer that God's word would never return back to Him void. She always told Nita and her other younger cousins that God couldn't lie and His word would always accomplish that which He sent it to do. That had to have been the furthest from Nita's truth at this point. Senior superlatives crowned her as most likeable. That must have been an accolade that expired the day you walked across the stage. She didn't have the juice any longer and clearly was far from being most wanted. More like "least wanted".

With absolutely no appetite of any size, Nita finally left the parking space she held hostage for hours and headed home in silence. Sleep wasn't a need at the moment, but she forced herself to plant her face in the two biggest plush pillows closest to the headboard. It was easier to sleep than constantly have a mind wondering what if, when, how, and why not. The pain was less bearable if she wasn't conscious to feel it. Just before she could plop down on the bed, a headache emerged. It was clearly time to tap into another world. She undressed to just her shirt and socks, threw the still turned off phone on her nightstand, and allowed the bed that held her many restless nights to do its best job. Comfort a hurting heart. Her sheets were the perfect kind of cold to sleep well into morning. No lavender essential oil was even needed this night. As sociable as she was, charging her iPhone wasn't on the list of importance. Prayerfully, a dream so grand would cause her to believe again. Something had to give. Her faith and hope had already given OUT.

Now that she'd agreed to be in Ashleigh's nuptials, this opened the door for constant wedding talk and "what do you think about this?" group text messages. She wondered, what in the world did she get herself into? Why didn't she suggest being a host rather than a bridesmaid? Again, totally different emotions based on the role. Was it too late to demote herself without being bombarded with the "whys" from Ashleigh and other friends? Nita did have a tendency of saying yes to too many obligations without thought. Would Ashleigh automatically assume jealousy was the reason? I mean, she didn't want it to be obvious of her wish to step down because of her own unhappiness with her marriage filing status.

She took a minute to think back on the many times she could have chosen to settle and possibly been married by now. Well, maybe not considering most guys who approached her were married, soon to be married, or definitely involved with another female. Nita chuckled under her breath as she thought back to the psychopath that was very much married with a child on the way who made it his point to walk over to her desk each and every morning and give her the compliment she secretly enjoyed. He was a short guy with a receding hairline who had all the confidence in the world plus Kanye West's. He was obsessed with Nita and was bold enough to invite her to his family reunion back in Ohio one summer. What a loser. Somehow they exchanged numbers and he didn't miss an evening messaging her once they had gotten home and settled in from work. My God did the attention he showed her come at the worst time. She was finally in a place where she was ready to move forward from her ex who had moved on a dozen times over at this point. She walked in the room daily with her shoulders back and head held high with much confidence knowing she deserved the world and some man was ready to give it to her or at least preparing himself. Just not a married man. Sigh.

After a while, the married man at work eventually left the company for a higher paying position at a neighboring firm. They kept in touch for maybe a month or so afterwards and it finally completely died. Sadly, the series of married or involved men continued on at her next place of business. Nita had finally been hired on at a mortgage firm about thirty minutes west of where she lived. This was definitely the spot to be for African Americans so you can already imagine the daily fashion show that Nita looked forward to participating in without question. A couple of months went by and Nita finally laid her eyes on a tall, chocolate drop who looked as though he played football or basketball, if not both sports, during his high school days. She finally got the courage to accidentally walk by his desk just to see what she might find lying around that would indicate if he was taken. What woman wasn't nosey? A wedding ring wasn't enough since most guys were likely not to wear theirs or couldn't help but be slick enough to leave it in the cup holder just before exiting their car.

Nita couldn't help but smile at the #1 Dad sponge finger sticking from behind his desktop. "Good father," she thought. "Definitely a win." He had a few pictures of a beautiful little mixed girl several places in his cubicle. She headed back to her seat before someone around him noticed she was snooping. Either that or he came back from his routine bathroom and ice machine break. That night she decided to take her time picking out her attire for the next day. It wasn't enough to be plain Jane with so many females on the second floor alone that could have his attention in a matter of seconds. Nita even slipped on her favorite hit playlist while rambling through tons of clothes and shoes in her overly crowded walk-in closet. Oh, and trust she had the perfect statement jewelry piece to go with any outfit of her choosing. Her sister didn't bother barging in her room to find out whom the latest crush was on. Nita twirled around the floor, throwing outfit after outfit in front of her body to see which particular combination matched the most and hugged her the best according to her vertical mirror. Just to be sure she also checked the vanity mirror. She had to be more than sure. For some reason, Nita was a sucker for a tall, chocolate drop. A good father combined was such a turn-on. I'm talking major turn-on for her.

An hour and a half had gone by and she finally put together the perfect parachute pants, red satin blouse, and leopard wedge heels that were bound to get his attention as soon as he laid eyes on her the next day. Oh, and he better be there the full day, she thought. No PTO of any kind needed to mess up this day.

The next morning she saw his black on black Camaro in her review mirror just as she merged to get off the exit. Because she was familiar with his daily routine of sitting in the car for at least twenty minutes, jammin' to the hottest mix on the local radio station, she took a quick right and headed to Chick-fil-A for chicken minis and hash browns. If her timing was right, they would end up at the revolving doors at the same time. The line wasn't too long for a Friday morning so she got her usual and headed to the call center. She didn't mind traveling three different interstates to get to the call center, simply because of the butterflies in her stomach she caught each and every day. As soon as she turned her right turning signal on to head into the parking lot, she noticed he had already backed his car into the closest parking space at the back of the call center's entrance. She sped up a little but not too much to where it was noticeable. Just after backing her car in, she double checked her lipstick, sprayed a little Miracle on her wrists and neck, and grabbed her precious Kate Spade bag and matching lunch box.

She took a quick peep in her rearview mirror and noticed he had opened the driver door and was preparing to make his way toward the revolving doors. Bingo. She had timed it just perfectly. She quickly jumped out of her car and headed down the sidewalk just in time to be in front of him as they met at the entrance. She smirked as though she didn't time this to perfection and proceeded into the first open slot in the revolving doors. She could see him eyeing her down. Not to mention she smelt delicious. Just as she pictured, he hurried through as though he was pushing the doors to move faster and caught up with her to start up a quick conversation. They headed to the cafeteria together. She didn't need a thing, but since she knew he had to have his coffee, ketchup for her hash browns was all of a sudden needed. He clearly was turned on by her high-waisted jeans, which happened to fit like a glove, and she couldn't help but love his tall frame. He wasn't the best-dressed man of the company by far; but boy did his charming confidence and skin tone make up for it. They made enough small talk for Nita to realize that he clearly wanted more. More conversation, and maybe even a small plate of Nita to-go.

She was certainly a confident woman, and in a class all by herself. She was never one to compare herself to other women or compete as though she wasn't the spot. She knew then she would pick things up right where they left off once they were both upstairs and settled into their desks. Since Instant Messenger may be a little distracting and obvious to anyone walking by, Nita decided to email him instead. He was the only guy with the last name Mobley so it was more than easy to find him in the company directory. The email system used was modern enough for her to see when he was logged in or away from his desk. She wasted no time in hitting 'Compose.' Her hash browns and chicken minis were getting colder by the minute. But there was no time to eat when a hot weekend date could be on the line at any moment. Nita was known to be an alpha female, but decided to ease into the conversation like an innocent high school cheerleader rather than going straight to the altar with this guy. Yep, at the altar in her white dress. But she knew what she wanted. Exactly what she wanted. She sent the first email asking how his usual breakfast spread was. Knots formed in the bottom of her tummy as she waited for a new message alert to pop on her screen.

At this point, that Chick-fil-A visit this morning was a waste. What girl could eat at this time? After seven long minutes, she finally got a reply. To her surprise, it wasn't the reply she anticipated, but at the same time, she kind of liked it. He answered her question as to how his breakfast was and the next sentence made her eyes widen within seconds. "What do you want from me? I've been through this a dozen times over. So let's cut to the chase, and tell me what you want from me?" Now Nita loved an aggressive man. In fact, that was top five on her list for the perfect guy. By no stretch of the imagination was she shy or timid. But now, the ball was in his court as to how this all played out. She didn't like that. Not one bit. He had the upper hand so she had to find a way of getting her hands on that ball again and dribbling it back into her court. Though she wanted to respond instantaneously, she had to think about a good reply. A reply that would leave him speechless, and thus give her the upper hand again.

She let him know that she peeped the way he ran his eyes down her body just before they reached the inside of the building. She also made sure that he knew that she knew he was feeling the girl. She noticed how she grabbed his attention any time she made a trip to the bathroom or returned from a team huddle. She knew that he purposely changed his route from lunch to ensure he passed her desk even though it was on the opposite side of the room, and that the office flirting was cute, but what about after hours? After expressing she knew the feelings were mutual, she decided to stroke his ego for a moment. Telling him that she noticed the pictures of a beautifully mixed, curly head girl who couldn't be more than four years old. That she could see herself with a good father and a strong, confident man like himself to take care of the two of them. She referenced two of them since only one child's daycare pics made it to his desk decorations. The trueness of that idea would soon be verified.

No doubt did Nita have confidence. It was a confidence that was always attractive and felt when in the presence of any male or female. She couldn't just come out and tell him how she felt though. She had a way with words, and always did. She didn't want to come off too strong so she decided to write him a letter. You read right, a letter, as an adult woman. After all, they were emailing on the company's watch so she didn't want to risk her nosey female team leader confronting her with print outs of anything said between the two of them. The job didn't pay six figures, but she sure needed every coin. Nita was enrolled as an adult student at the local college taking courses four nights a week. She decided to use the time her Theology instructor spent rambling to draft her letter to Mr. Mobley. Now, it wasn't going to be a four-page letter like Aaliyah described in her hit single, but it was surely going to be enough words and paragraphs to get her point across. That evening in class, Nita attention span to focus was probably the worst it had been all semester.

Since she maintained a B-average she could afford to look as though she was writing notes while putting all of her emotions and feelings on paper. Her neighbor tried looking over his shoulder a few times wondering what she was writing, since Mrs. Newcomb wasn't saying much of anything note-taking worthy. He was known for being nosey and invading her space from time to time since the semester began. Fortunately for Nita, finals were next week and she'd probably never have another course with the nosey fella. Nita ignored him and continued with her "love" letter to Mr. Mobley. Once again she mentioned her admiration of him being a good father and how rare that seemed to be amongst African American men today. She stroked his ego a little further than the work email and decided to let him know that she could see them being a couple. He was also a Christian man who believed in God, which was an even bigger turn-on and top priority for her ideal list. She decided not to shy away from the fact that she wanted whatever this "thing" was between the two of them to go beyond the four walls of the call center. More like the four walls of an all brick six-bedroom home, three-car garage, charcoal cabinets, and walk-in closets but who was imagining?

He was a standup guy and after the bad apples she'd experienced over the years, she could appreciate him for that. In her mind, she could see their little family prepping for Sunday morning worship, matching outfits, and of course the Sunday afternoon throw down in the kitchen. A typical Sunday fun day. All her life, she was a sucker for a good father. Surely that was her way of dealing with an absent father who had no dealings with her at all. Notably, following receipt and reading of her letter, Mr. Mobley indirectly made it clear he had other thoughts in mind for the two that were on a much more temporary basis. Nita wasn't up for being any man's sidepiece so she decided to back completely off and show Mr. Mobley no attention whatsoever. From that day forward, he never existed.

After the last workplace crush with Mr. Mobley that didn't go according to plan, Nita decided to let it go and "do her". That notion was pretty short lived as a new money-laundering department came to vacate the empty section to the right of her team. The first few days she noticed a few African American men but didn't think too much of it. She was over workplace eye candy. On the other hand, her neighbor who lived and craved for male attention was sure to make herself friendly. She had to have been about fifteen years older than Nita but could eat attention from male and female for breakfast, lunch, and dinner. It was quite sickening and embarrassing most days. Hence the reason Nita never left home without her headphones. Her turn the volume up and tune out game was mighty strong. She had a teenage daughter so maybe that was the reason behind the immaturity she displayed at the office daily. Before she knew it, they were going to lunch together and hanging out after work. Nita went day by day with her headphones in ear and Pandora on blast as she'd always done. In fact, her processing timeframes may have even increased. That's how unbothered she was of this new group of men being close to her workspace.

After a while, she noticed the chocolate guy, who was easy on the eye and had a wardrobe that was more than attractive, seemed to want her attention. This was sadly nothing new for her. Many men wanted Nita's attention. Very few knew what to do with it once she served it on a silver platter and delivered it to their doorstep. So, Nita decided to play the game with him. But this time, the ball would be and remain in her court. Before she humiliated herself again, she confirmed with another friend that sat in the area if it was obvious he wanted her attention. When that friend noticed he stared at her often, she decided to make the first move to let him know, she knew. He worked a different schedule than Nita but every evening before leaving the office, he was always sure to come around and give his goodbyes. And of course one last look at Nita before he hopped on the elevator and hurried out of the parking lot. It was flattering for her to say the least. God had to know that it wasn't easy dodging attention as a woman. Nita didn't crave it, but she certainly didn't deny her enjoyment of it when it was presented. She didn't have to guess if he was interested. Oh, honey, it was obvious at this point.

She let his "staring" phase go on for a few days before she decided to make the first move. Normally, she would wait on the male to do so. But every now and then, the woman wants to assume the dominant role. Nita just so happened to do so back to back. It was three fifty-two in the afternoon and Nita knew Mr. Ballard would be preparing to leave shortly. She could hear the chatter and small talk between him and his colleagues over the wall of her cubicle. He had a good way of smiling and showing all of those pearly whites as he stood to stretch with his face in Nita's direction. She peeped game every time. This day, Nita decided to signal for him to come to her with a head motion. He did so immediately, as if he was waiting on this day with much anticipation. She scribbled her number on a piece of sticky-note paper and handed it to him. He smiled back, showing every single tooth as though he was preparing for a dental X-ray. "You've been wanting this right?" Nita asked.

Just when she thought his smile couldn't get any larger, it expanded as he winked at her and walked off. Yep, he wanted her. Now to see how long it takes for him to use it. From the looks of that smile, she wouldn't make it out the parking lot before her phone rang. By the time Nita made it out the door and to the top of the parking lot, her phone rang from an unknown number just as the light turned green signaling her to turn. She answered in her most professional tone as though she had not a clue who it could be. She prayed he couldn't feel her smile through the phone. She was blushing times ten. But it was actually cool since it was obvious over the last few weeks that he showed interest first. They talked for what seemed like forever until he pulled up at the gym. Nita hadn't talked to anyone besides mama or granny on her way home from work in forever. Actually, never. It was either the thirty-minute conversations with the two of them or listening to the five o' clock traffic jam mix on the local radio station. She felt butterflies just at the thought of a male voice on the other end. Clearly there was a need to spend some extra time laying out tomorrow's attire. Texting during the day and the normal after work phone call became their normal. Things got even better as Mr. Ballard made it a point each day to find out what Nita wanted for lunch and breakfast. Her other teammates were jealous to say the least. She loved it. He had no children, drove a nice two-door sports car, and made a pretty hefty salary. Needless to say, bringing a bagged lunch was never the case for him, which meant every day Nita had a choice of eating somewhere different since he never excluded her when it came to his lunch plans. She always declined, but her work homegirls always tried to get their order in and pretend it was for Nita.

He had a turquoise button up that became Nita's favorite for him to wear. He even smelt divine with new cologne each day. Because she loved that particular blue, he made it a point to wear different designs if not have that color thrown in his tie somewhere. The attention he showed her at work was everything she always wanted. He noticed everything about her and was sure to compliment her every single day. He loved her confidence, and she loved his attention, which seemed to be tailor-made just for her. She couldn't change a toenail color without him noticing seconds before the elevator door closed. That's how much attention to detail he showed concerning anything with Nita.

One day, Nita's attention seeking neighbor decided to start up a conversation with her just as she was about to put her head-buds in her ear. Nita rolled her eyes without the woman noticing. "Guess I wasn't fast enough," she thought. Ms. Ware decided to mention going to lunch with the guys on the team adjacent to theirs. Of course she had also witnessed all of the attention Mr. Ballard was showing her. A little jealous was she? Nita wouldn't put anything past that girl. She came across as if shady was her middle name in this life and another life. The little envious, older woman couldn't wait to let Nita know that Mr. Ballard was no single man by any means.

"Have you seen his pretty girlfriend? She is super gorgeous with the prettiest shape."

Nita's stomach seemed to have quenched a bit as though she was on the largest rollercoaster at the old amusement park a few miles down the road. She couldn't be talking about her Mr. Ballard. Nita pretended as though she wasn't sure whom the nosey neighbor was referencing. The other guy who accompanied him on lunch was definitely not dating a woman so whom else could she be referring to? Nita was wise enough to not let an ounce of emotion or concern register on her face. Let's be honest, she was talking with a messy, older female and she wouldn't dare give her the satisfaction.

"That's nice. I'm sure she's beautiful," Nita responded.

Humph. She had to really have been born last night if she thought she was getting any kind of reaction that day. Nita knew she would have this resolved in the next hour as her shift was coming to an end. She decided to take a different approach today just in case the news received was true. Rather than wait for his normal incoming call, Nita decided to give him a call just as soon as she could get in the car and reach for the seatbelt. After about three rings, he answered. His voice led her to believe he knew that a little birdie dropped some information today that couldn't be taken back. Nita was on a mission and had no time to be playing with guys who thought at any point that it was okay to desire her attention and have a whole girlfriend back at home. She cut straight to the chase and let him in on the unexpected news she received today.

To her surprise, he didn't admit it as the truth but chose to stay in silence for a few moments. After several minutes, he finally informed Nita that he didn't know how to tell her. He really enjoyed their conversing daily and didn't want that to stop. Fortunately, this was somewhat fresh so Nita didn't trip too badly. She did ask why in the world he wanted her attention when he had a gorgeous girlfriend who happened to be a dancer with a body second to none. He wanted Nita to know that her confidence was very attractive and his girlfriend apparently didn't have much of that. Even with a physique, perfect skin tone, and length of hair that would have any other female envious. Strangely, Nita felt this as somewhat even more flattering that he was very well taken but showed her the attention of a girlfriend just as much. What she wasn't down for was being anyone's "work" girlfriend. Just thinking of her neighbor being right made her stomach turn. How would she hide this considering everyone around her and his work buddies could clearly tell there was something there?

As time went on, nothing changed. He still sought her attention, offered to buy her breakfast and lunch, and even called after work as though she never knew of his relationship status. Nita thought she could cut it off without second thoughts. But for whatever reason, she enjoyed his companionship a lot. She knew it could go no further than work so continuing on didn't seem like much of a big deal. Sadly enough, in the back of her mind she knew she was cheating herself. She deserved to be some man's everything, and what he could give her wasn't even a fraction of what she deserved. How bad did this grieve God? Nita seemed to have a thing for allowing pint people to give her what only gallon level individuals possessed. It's funny that Mr. Ballard was attracted to her confidence. Meanwhile Nita had no idea of how God saw her. She clearly needed a new prescription for her lenses if she wanted to see herself even close to the way God saw her.

Mr. Ballard had been off for a few days so the communication between he and Nita was limited to say the least. Maybe this was God's way of removing her from this worthless relationship since Nita wasn't willing to do so on her own. As long as he was engaging in any form of flirting or communication with her, she would always reply back. Upon his return back to the office, Nita could hear claps from his entire team as he made his way to his desk that morning. She didn't receive a text asking what she wanted for breakfast from downstairs but she brushed it off. She didn't even bother to eavesdrop to see what all the hype was about. Instead, she cut put her head-buds in her hair per usual, and turned the most recently played Pandora station up to the max. At this point she didn't care if it was a distraction for her cubicle neighbors. It was just one of those days.

Later that day, Nita's neighbor who sat adjacent to her, decided to let her know the noise they all heard earlier was in regards to Mr. Ballard's recent proposal to his girlfriend. She knew he was going on vacation but had no idea bending down on one knee and asking the girlfriend whom he didn't feel was very confident to marry him. The same girlfriend he didn't mind embarrassing while at work giving his attention to another. Wow. That seemed to have been all Nita knew to cut whatever it was left the two of them could possibly have. The flirting and back and forth of who could get whose attention was played out and expired at this point. Nita was good at pretending as though one didn't exist. Besides, her nosey neighbor had witnessed this cold shoulder just about daily. God sure did have a funny way about getting her attention and this time he was speaking loud and clear. Glancing in his direction was no longer apart of her day. She was definitely humiliated. The office seemed so much quieter each day now that the two of them were no longer "friends". Although the feelings didn't go outside of the office, it was still frustrating, considering the incident with Mr. Mobley wasn't too far back. Any chances of getting involved with any other man in that call center were completely done. Her neighbor chose to brag of her lunch dates with Mr. Mobley and his colleagues after realizing their little fling had come to a shocking end. Nita was definitely not studdin' her one bit and that was okay. She may have been a Christian but it was nothing for her to act as though you didn't exist no matter your proximity to her. It was time for a mental detox and not having anyone eyeing, pursuing, or after her attention was the perfect way to begin day one of the detox. Nita went through similar issues in high school with catty women so she knew the benefits of clearing one's mind and dedicating needed time to focus on her well-being specifically was. In some ways Nita couldn't help but believe it was actually kind of sweet knowing that God cared about her way too much to allow her to settle or be someone's second best. That in itself made her smile. A smile that was felt inwardly before displayed outwardly.

Nita was reminded of the story of Hannah. Hannah had no child and was very grieved. Though she desperately desired a child, she could not conceive. Nita could relate since she desperately desired a helpmeet, a husband, a companion, and the ultimate husband. Hannah was one of two wives and the other wife taunted Hannah concerning her barrenness. No one taunted Nita about being single besides the little voices in her head. Even at holiday gatherings, she wasn't forced with dozens of family members asking when she would tie the knot. One could only imagine not being able to conceive and then being mocked because of it. What's ironic about this story is the fact that Hannah was loved greatly by her husband. In fact, he bestowed richer gifts upon her than he did upon his other wife. With all that Elkanah was giving her, a double portion, she was still unfulfilled. Hannah was childless. And in that time, it was considered a curse if you did not have a child(ren). She was not producing and Peninnah was producing all the time, over and over. Can you imagine sharing a man and having the other woman's children running around all day while your womb is barren? You probably would just find you another man, right? Tears well in the bottom of my eyes at even the thought of it.

Can you imagine the feelings of inadequacy and feeling forgotten by God? As though you had some ugly visible birthmark and everyone around you was just as normal as possible. This must have been beyond difficult, especially when you've lived a life holy and acceptable unto God. She longed for a son out of her own womb to love and nurture. As the years went by, her agony became more intense, and her barrenness was a greater burden because of the jealousy and envy that accompanied her heart. It didn't make it any better that Peninnah frequently tantalized Hannah for being childless. Can you imagine the difficulty of living with a nasty woman like Peninnah? There was a place for women like her and it rhymes with "six feet under". You can probably hear her teasing, "Look at my babies over here. Aren't they precious? They look just like their handsome father. Why don't you have any babies, Mrs. Hannah? Huh?" She thought she was one upping Hannah since they were sleeping with the same man who was producing the same seed, yet she had what Hannah yearned for. Peninnah had no idea that she was provoking Hannah according to God's plans though she

assumed it was out of her own flesh. This was God's way
of bringing Hannah to a place in which she needed to be for
birthing what was soon to come from her womb. It would
be easy to gather assumptions of what Hannah must have
felt in this situation and the distrust she may held in her
heart toward God. How could he allow this situation to
fester over time when Hannah had been faithful to Him?
Yet and still, Hannah cried out to God, which was all too
familiar for Nita.

Though childless, Hannah was not prayer-less. The
enemy may have wanted to strangle her neck and tape her
mouth shut, but he couldn't. There was a sound in her belly
that was getting prepared to sound the alarm. She earnestly
and silently prayed to God day after day. On the contrary,
Peninnah pushed her right into a place of prayer. And this
wasn't just some ordinary prayer. It was a prayer that
would reach Heaven and cause God to move and do so
quickly. Besides, He was behind the scenes orchestrating
every single scene like a muppet show anyway. He knew
there was a certain cry that Hannah needed to make in
order for Him to come see about her barrenness. What's
strange is that Hannah's prayer was never geared toward
God making Peninnah suffer or punishing her for the way

she'd mocked Hannah's barrenness. Hannah didn't pray that Peninnah's joy might be less or her egotistical behavior would disappear. She didn't pray that God's vengeance destroy her and move she and her children out of the home she shared with their husband. This prayer was totally about her own sorrows and God coming to her rescue. At this point, it wasn't about Peninnah. It wasn't about Elkanah. Hannah wanted God to give her what was due to her. The very thing that had her name signed on the deed. She stopped looking at everyone else and said, "God, it's me. I want what you want me to have and nothing more or less. I'm not getting up from this place until you stop playing and speak to me."

Hannah stayed on her face and prayed until God started speaking. She wasn't about any games at this point. During her days of crying out, Hannah promised God that if He would give her a son, she would dedicate him to God. She got up from that place of praying and the Bible says when she finished praying, her countenance was no more sad. Just thinking of the sobbing and travailing and idea of being totally naked with God hiding nothing is enough to give one chills. A rag was probably more needed than the finest box of Kleenex. Hannah had had enough of being tormented and watching Peninnah birth children as she silently watched with a barren womb. She eventually received God's promise and bore a son named Samuel whose name means, "Asked of God." God remembered Hannah. Ironically, God blessed her with more than just the one son she desired. He blessed her immeasurably more with three more sons and two daughters. Her story gives us insight into God's heart. It wasn't that her desires were ungodly by any means. In fact, He placed the longing for a child in her heart Himself.

Nita eventually rocked asleep the baby of being married and having a complete family. What grieved her most was thinking back on promises God had given her through many mouthpieces on Earth. Her former first lady was responsible for women's fellowship one particular month. She decided to assign the few young women in the church a specific woman from the Bible. As hoped for, Nita was assigned Ruth. She immediately felt this had to be a sign straight from Heaven concerning what was about to take place in her life that she had been waiting anxiously for many years now. Her first lady explained what she was looking for with this study and that if the Lord led her to, she would discuss why she assigned each young adult that particular woman. Nita had heard this story dozens of times over the years but never thought enough to go in depth with studying it out. All she cared about was the excitement that came from a special woman who was privileged with the perfect love story and was eventually found by an amazing man. Yes, she was found and didn't seek the man or try and convince him that she was the right one for him. Nita didn't waste time studying out her virtuous woman, as she was eager to know what else could possibly be learned to make this story any more beautiful. Ruth was a woman who remained loyal to her mother-in-law Naomi after the death of her husband and in-laws. Though Naomi decided to return to her home, Ruth insisted on staying with her. In this day and age Nita found this strange due to the fact that when the relationship has ended, even though in this case was due to death, you don't find the woman sticking around with the mindset Ruth had. Maybe for a little while to help with the grief, but Ruth seemed to be indebted to Naomi even when she wasn't entitled to be. She could have very well stuck around long enough for it to not be awkward and then parted ways to continue her journey to healing. This story was definitely unusual for Nita's day and age. Later on Nita learned that Ruth gleaned in the fields of Naomi's relative Boaz whom out of compassion and obedience allowed Ruth to glean but also purposely made sure extra grain was left just for her. This particular part of the love story left butterflies circling every wall of Nita's belly as she never witnessed a man go to such lengths without ever having even a two-minute conversation. As if it wasn't strange enough that Ruth was following her mother-in-law to her homeland, Ruth obeyed Naomi's commands of seeking marriage with Boaz. Ummmmmm, can we say awkward? Ruth was once married to her son and more than likely head-over-heels in love with him and though dead, his mother is insisting Ruth marries another man. In the end, the get married and conceive a son after another man technically had first dibs.

After Nita presented her character, she waited anxiously, unable to focus on the others presenting. All she could think was maybe her first lady could spill the beans and confirm what she had hoped in her spirit. That her God-sent mate would show up any day now. After another hour, her first lady asked if young adults could line up along the altar and she began to anoint their heads with oil. Nita's anxiety rose to another level. This was surely a day that was journal worthy. She was about four people down and had no other choice but to wait her turn. Twenty minutes later, her first lady was finally standing in front of her ready to release what God gave her. By this time Nita's palms were sweating and she prayed silently that her first lady didn't try and hold her hands while praying. She released revelation as to why God gave her Ruth for the woman Nita was to speak on. Her first words were "Boaz is coming in this season." She then went on to compliment Nita on taking her daughter to Disney World and forcing her to think beyond North Carolina. Her first lady then went on to explain that Nita's Disney World was her future husband's local theme park. That Ruth Chris would be their cheapest date and this man thought on a whole different level. She encouraged Nita over and over to never settle and be privy to the men who were coming that would look as though they were the "one," but would not be. She encouraged Nita to have a strong prayer life and ask God for a strong spirit of discernment so that when the wrong one presented himself, she wouldn't mistake him for being Boaz.

You can imagine the tears that left Nita's eyes like the largest rainfall. Everything she had desired in her spirit was just prophesied to her. A few weeks prior to this women's fellowship, the mother of the church pulled Nita aside one Sunday following service and told Nita she had a vision of her coming down the aisle on her wedding date. She bragged of how beautiful Nita was and assured her that when the day came, she would look back and come to her with excitement reminiscing on the day she told Nita about the vision. After an amazing gathering that turned into hours, the mother of the church was sure to speak with Nita to remind her of what she spoke that day and what was revealed on that day. By this time Nita was so beyond full on a restored hope. She needed that day more than anything. All she could think was the word season and her first lady whom she trusted with her life spoke that her Boaz was coming in "this" season. She had to prepare and prepare quick. In her eyes seasons weren't years. They were a few months if that. In her mind, she wouldn't leave her house another day without preparing herself as if she would meet him on any given day. It had been years since Nita engaged in a relationship of any kind. Her sister made jokes about how certain body parts probably didn't work the same anymore since it had been so long since Nita was sexually active.

Fortunately, that didn't faze Nita one bit. She was determined to set the best example for other women and having men in and out of her life just wasn't going to be a reality. She believed in being a role model at all costs even if that meant forsaking her flesh and holding out until the right man stepped up. Nita may not have grew up in a two-parent home but she still believed a whole family was possible if she did her part and showed God she would trust Him even on days when she couldn't locate Him. Nita witnessed so many other women her age who settled just to have help with bills or a man they could brag about on social media in order to appear as though they had it all together. It wasn't easy by far. But settling was something she could never do in any area of her life.

For years, Nita felt her season of singleness was extended and the lease was renewed without ever signing the consent letter as the tenant. As you can see, she had her share of forcibly being the controller of time. Even after all of her experiences and disappointments she experienced after attempting to do what only God could do, she still chose to download a dating app her close friend had success with. To her surprise, the app would not let her sign in successfully no matter what she tried. Talk about a sign from God. She finally came to terms with the reality that time can be an enemy or opportunity. This enemy causes us to become discouraged and quit. It forces one to look at the promise and deem it unnecessary to accomplish. Most of us have made it to be the enemy. Has your misconception of time caused you to abort a baby in its early stages because you weren't aware of a beating heart? What would happen if you embraced time?

***

Hebrews 10:35-36 (AMP): *"Do not, therefore, fling away your fearless confidence, for it carries a great and glorious compensation of reward. For you have need of steadfast patience and endurance, so that you may perform and fully accomplish the will of God, and thus receive and carry away [and enjoy to the full] what is promised."*

Luke 1:45 (KJV)*: And blessed is she that believed: for there shall be a performance of those things which were told her from the Lord.*

What Big Momma Said

But seek ye first the kingdom of God, and his righteousness;
and all these things shall be added unto you. (Matthew 6:33)(KJV)
Love the Lord your God with all your heart and with all your
soul and with all your mind and with all your strength.
(Mark 12:30)(NIV)

The phone rings.

"Ma'am," Michelle said.

"Well, hey granny's baby. How are you today? By the tone of your voice, you're still in the valley," Big Momma said with a grin in her voice that showed through the phone.

Michelle immediately rolled her eyes. If anybody called, rest assured that granny was calling. And she was well mature in her Christian walk to not sugarcoat anything, even for her oldest grandchild. Although granny didn't take pleasure in hearing her granddaughter defeated, she couldn't help but chuckle at the fact the devil had that much power over her. Not to mention, she was just on the mountaintop only about three days ago. This was an ongoing cycle and all granny wanted was for her adult grandchild to recognize the tactics of the enemy. He uses the same tactics each and every time and even the same people to get Michelle in the dumps.

"I'm alright."

Big Momma knew she was far from all right. And Michelle knew also, but didn't want to admit it considering Big Momma was always right. Michelle was never too excited about that. It was normal for granny to spoon feed Michelle encouragement for various reasons. Many days Michelle found herself on the mountaintop, excited about life and the things God revealed to her supernaturally. On those days, she couldn't wait to get home and share with granny knowing she would be all ears. These are the conversations that normally went past an hour until the point where one of them said, "Okay, I have to go now." What almost seemed like a few hours timeframe, the enemy would come like a thief in the night and steal every ounce of joy the purpose-filled girl ever had. Just thinking about it makes me angry because everyone around her knows the calling God has for her life. She once heard the phrase, "Thieves don't break into empty homes." Clearly, she was loaded the way the enemy stayed on her trail. In fact, none of her friends faced as much opposition as she did. It was always something happening. Normal conversations often geared towards telling of something totally off the wall happening. She was loaded, and the enemy knew it. If he could stop her in her trails, he knew that he was also holding up deliverance, healing, and freedom for dozens of other girls. You better believe he wasn't going to lighten up.

While many children her age had lost their grandparents in their earlier years of living, Michelle had a very unique and close relationship with her granny. She was the one grandchild who spoke with her grandmother every single day. He was kind enough to send her a granny like Sadie. She was the oldest of all grandchildren and sometimes felt as if her mistakes were to save them from falling into some of the same pits. She considered it an important task to set the best example for her younger cousins, whether any of them ever realized that or not. Miss Sadie was the normal type of granny. You know, who worried nonstop about her children and twice more about her grands and great grands. It was extreme. Extreme as in, she had to receive a call from Michelle every evening to confirm she made it in from work safely. She wanted to be contacted immediately following any doctor visits to ensure everything went smoothly. Extreme as in, if there was a car accident on 85N and Michelle travelled seventy-four, Miss Sadie called to make sure she was okay. At times, it may have seemed annoying to those who didn't understand the nature of their relationship. Not to mention, Michelle had a very old soul as well. But for Michelle, it was everything. She cherished their relationship with everything in her. So much so that she even debated recording some of their conversations so that in the event granny reached Heaven before she did, she would always have the privilege of hearing her voice again.

Big Momma was always the first person Michelle or any other grandchildren for that matter called in times of trouble. They knew she could get a prayer to Heaven quicker than a teenager to a party on a Friday night. Seconds after their parents left the driveway to head out of town. Michelle had witnessed it firsthand. In her middle school days, her grandmother was due to get married to an amazing man. He made her giggle like Michelle had never seen before. At times, it had to have been the cutest thing to watch seeing her grandmother smile and carry herself like a schoolgirl dating the most popular quarterback of the local high school. If she could imagine anything inwardly,

Michelle would be sure to see butterflies swarming the walls of her grandmother's belly. What a beautiful sight to see. One day, this smile and schoolgirl-like ambiance would change. While visiting his hometown one weekend, the man who made her grandmother smile like no other suffered a heart attack and was found dead in the house he planned to vacate soon. Michelle was so used to seeing her grandmother with an upbeat attitude that it broke her to pieces seeing her down in the dumps. Sadly, there was nothing Michelle could do to relieve the pain. Only God could heal this wound.

She tried to make the best of this tragic incident but her countenance had changed which made it more than obvious to pick up on her spirit when in her presence. What's strange is one morning her grandmother saw dozens of black birds in her backyard. The same backyard she and the man of her dreams had planned to wed in. It was the perfect space for what would be a beautiful ceremony. Black birds were known to symbolize death. Her grandmother was notorious for her visions and dreams but it never occurred to them that death would strike so close to home. From that day forward, Michelle and her sister would stay each weekday night with her grandmother as a means of comfort since their mother worked third shift. Michelle was never one to sleep alone so she cuddled up with her grandmother every single night. She could remember her grandmother getting out of bed in the wee hours of the night and getting on her knees to pray. Some nights, she would lay prostrate on the floor and just cry out to God. To this day, any time Michelle hears her grandmother praying, her eyes wail within seconds. Her words carried so much weight. So much power. Just being in her presence while she cried out to God was enough to give anyone chills. Many days Michelle wondered if she would ever be the type of woman who could travail in the spirit and cause mountains to move. She admired her grandmother and her strength more than any other woman on the face of this earth, which is why though she didn't always enjoy chastisement from her, she knew it was beneficial for her in this walk of life.

There was one special quality her grandmother possessed outside of her anointing. This happened to be her wisdom. In Michelle's mind, she would need to be the age of her grandmother if not soon approaching to even bring that type of wisdom into her possession. No matter whom it concerned, or the magnitude of the offense or situation, her grandmother refused to allow bitterness to ever take root in her life. So much so that she would make herself apologize even if she wasn't the one in wrongdoing just to prevent the enemy from seeping in anywhere. He was never invited in her life. Ever been around someone that seemed to do most things right and never held grudges? Always spoke to people even if the person(s) they were speaking to didn't actually care for them? That one person who always tends to shut down comments that have negative written all over them? That was Big Momma. Contrary to popular belief, they do exist huh? It's quite interesting that Michelle felt she needed to be at least over fifty to ever be in a place of maturity to carry herself the way her grandmother does. Michelle wasn't quite there yet, and her grandmother wasn't going to stroke her ego and pat her on the back to get her there either. She was hard on Michelle, and for good reasoning too. It was all done through love. Michelle shared many things with her granny that most grandchildren would shy away from ever telling. She had no problem being open with her because if anything, the truth was going to be delivered and never diluted in any way. Fasting and prayer was always her grandmother's two-piece combo when it came to defeating any enemy.

She was something like a modern day David who had no problem conquering any Goliath even on her worse day.

One of the most frustrating things for Michelle was seeing a preview of her future only to have it end in her face within a matter of seconds. Oddly enough, she continuously saw the same preview over and over that she would travel the world encouraging the masses, have a loving husband who was designed specifically for her, and break the generational curses bestowed on their family. She had seen the same preview so many times that she cried out to God and asked Him to please put an end to confirming things that weren't manifesting in the natural. Yes, she was bold enough to ask God to stop. Seeing things in the spirit definitely had its perks, but this also discouraged her. Ironically, the verifications only increased after she softly whispered her request for them to be discontinued. Confirmations only revealed the distance between what He revealed supernaturally and what she saw physically. When you've received the same revelations year after year without it being brought into fruition, you would probably become dismayed as well. She wanted a tangible manifestation of His promises. Was this too hard to ask from a God who could do the impossible? She wondered.

Like the Big Momma she was, she shut down thoughts of disbelief before Michelle could even get her feelings in words off her lips. She reminded Michelle that God was and still is committed to His promises concerning her. He is committed to justice. He is committed to making right that which was wrong. His word can never return to Him void. He would redeem her if she would only stand and do her part, which did not include becoming bitter during the process. This was certainly easier said than done, especially when it seemed like those around her were obtaining the promises and she was left to watch enviously. The more she whined to Big Momma, the more she explained that Michelle had no idea how people were behind closed doors or even how they obtained what they had. That was more so in reference to obtaining things out of the will of God. For the most part they were good at making the reality look much more glamourous than it actually was. She was saddened by lifestyles that were only an illusion. At times, this certainly frustrated Michelle. It was as though her feelings had no significance when she wanted Big Momma to side with her. Big Momma wasn't here for it. On the opposite side, she had enough discernment to recognize immediately this was nothing but a trick of the enemy, and he was a liar.

Big Momma could also tell stories for days. No matter the subject, every anecdote had a significant meaning and life lesson associated with it. There was one story in particular Michelle could always remember vividly hearing her grandmother tell of it. There was a little boy with his mother at a local store where her grandmother happened to be shopping at. As the two maneuvered throughout the store, the little boy asked persistently for a hardball piece of candy. The little boy could have been no more than six years old. He pulled the little kid game of asking over and over until eventually the parent gives in and says 'yes' out of aggravation. With every "please" he shouted, his mother had a stern "no" to dish back. This went on for several moments. The store wasn't too busy so Michelle's grandmother could hear the back and forth between the mother and son easily. Eventually, the mother decided rather than continue back and forth with her son as if they possessed the same level of power, she would teach him a lesson that was sure to hush his mouth for the remainder of the day. Literally. As soon as he yelled out another "please," she would give in and hand over the hardball candy. He waited a few seconds and asked, "please" again. The mother handed it over while trying not to explode from laughing. If he ever learned a lesson, today would be the day. The little boy wasted no time popping the wrapper off with the single top tooth he still managed to have. Within seconds, he was screaming, "Hot, hot, hot," while running around in circles uncontrollably. Finally, he spit the red fire ball out which rolled down aisle five under the dividers. His mother knew the hotness of the candy was nothing to play with. But since the little boy insisted, now seemed to be the appropriate time to prove that everything we desire may not necessarily be good for us. Not to mention, someone else knows best and can tell you rather than watching you go through unnecessary inconveniences.

Every time Michelle decides to go off on a tangent begging God, "Please, please, please. I want, I want, I want." Big Momma kindly brings that story up as if it was on scheduled queue. Understanding the right thing released at the wrong time can feel more like a curse than a blessing was a huge lesson Big Momma was sure to teach Michelle whether class was in session or not. The Lord is able to scan the timeline of your entire life. In essence, He knows precisely when you're ready and mature for various blessings, experiences, opportunities, and relationships. Every lesson she wished to teach didn't always have to be tied back to the Bible but always had a viable reference as it relates to character.

Without realizing, Michelle would dial her grandmother's number at the moment she needed to vent or felt herself on the verge of a breakdown. Of course she could talk to God but it was something about getting the concerns of her heart in the ear of her grandmother. She knew that her grandmother could hold the weight of her shoulders and not buckle no matter the magnitude. Crying hysterically before her grandmother could utter even a "hello" could summarize dozens of their conversations. But one thing for sure, Big Momma never came down off the word. She intentionally drilled into Michelle's mind that the enemy was not going to play games when it came to what he wished to devour. Michelle. He wasn't going to sit back and watch while a red carpet is laid out for Michelle to walk on as she walked the road to gaining stored up blessings. Regardless of what Michelle felt and how badly she wished to wallow in self-pity, her grandmother persistently and without invitation made it plain as day for her. She encouraged Michelle to stand on the promises of

God and His word. Even if she only had one scripture to stand on, she persuaded her to speak that same scripture over and over. Big Momma knew that Michelle was carrying a heavy pound baby in the spirit that would surely deliver masses of women. She was concerned and wished for Michelle to understand that in order to birth a healthy baby, she had to intake healthy things. In essence, fear, doubt, past disappointments, bitterness, and un-forgiveness could never be a part of her diet if she wished to give birth to a healthy child.

Not only did Big Momma tell good stories and always have a word of encouragement up her sleeve, she could also sing a tune every now and then. She used to sing a song and the lyrics went something like this, "You need to wait, wait, on the Lord and be of good courage. 'Cause He will strengthen my heart." Nah, granny. He's weakening my heart by the day, she thought, coupled with an eye roll. Regardless of the day or the hour, Big Momma had a way of making Michelle see the bigger picture in every adversity faced, especially waiting for God's best. She repeatedly affirmed the fact that God does all things well in His timing so it's best to sit back and enjoy the journey. For very soon, you'll hold the promise in your arms and the pain of the pregnancy will no longer matter. Countless days Michelle could have thrown in the towel, but her grandmother's wisdom and love kept her on the straight and narrow with strength to hold on a little while longer. If it were up to granny she would live and not die, and especially not to bitterness. Not on Big Momma's watch.

Baggage Claim

Casting all your cares [all your anxieties, all your worries, and all your concerns, once and for all] on Him, for He cares about you [with deepest affection, and watches over you very carefully].
(I Peter 5:7)(AMP)

We are troubled on every side, yet not distressed; we are perplexed, but not in despair; Persecuted, but not forsaken; cast down, but not destroyed (II Corinthians 4:8-9)(KJV)

"Bag lady, you gone hurt your back, dragging all them bags like that."*

Oh, so you decided to sing along as well huh? Now I understand what Erykah Badu meant when she sang those lyrics. Little did I know, one day those bags would really get in my way. The bags of bitterness attached themselves to my shoulders like an aggravating mosquito on a hot, July summer afternoon. To be honest, those bags had gotten in my way for the umpteenth time. And I was sick of them. Did I have the strength to unpack 'em?

"Look at your neighbor. Tell your neighbor: this is the year I get healed and whole," Pastor Bynum declared as she presented her sermon title to the congregation. It was

January first of the year of victory and the crowd yelled and clapped as a sign of agreement with what just left the pastor's lips. This shaking of excitement in the room led Jennifer to believe she must not be the only one bound and in need of healing. Physical healing wasn't on her prayer list, but total deliverance from past hurt and people sure was.

On the outside, Jennifer had it all together, and I do mean "all together". She sure had a good way of hiding all of that, which was easy to fool most out of view. From the way she posted inspirational messages on social media, to the perfection of her lipstick and liner, and even the way she wore her hair and dressed so stylish. Her messy bun and sweats type days still had a way of making her look so innocent, but yet gorgeous. Unlike others, this girl surely had it all together and couldn't possibly need much. On the outside, everything was all together. On the inside, everything was all out of place. You know, like milk in the cabinets, frozen meat in the refrigerator, big breasts in an A-cup bra, and so on. You get my point.

Even still, she was looked at by the world as the epitome of a woman who made no mistakes, had no insecurities, and lived in perfect paradise. She was the type of chick you saw in magazines or walking the runway with the fiercest walk in New York Fashion week. NOT. Tears ran down her face like rivers of water when Pastor Bynum conducted the altar call. She found herself in the center of this message crying out inwardly for help. The ugly cry that involved sobs that quickly turned into loud weeping. Sort of like the help needed in the most popular horror film that forced everyone to the edge of their seats as they waited for a horrible murder to take place. The audience knew something major had to occur to shift how the movie ended. Yes, that's the type of help she needed and even yearned for. This needed help forced words to be written in her stylish journal night after night. She could write freely withholding nothing knowing judgement couldn't take place. But the help she needed wasn't enough to cause her to step out of the aisle and make her way to the altar.

Oh, nah. She couldn't risk someone in the congregation assuming she needed any help from the Most High. Remember, her church members were also friends on social media. So they saw the life she displayed online. She had no other choice for the two to be synonymous. Miss Independent was her nickname. She had been around this mountain of bitterness far too long. She didn't need another prophecy, another encouraging text message, or positive Facebook status to read. The silent frustrations of winter caught up with her and now, she wanted total healing and HEALING alone. Unfortunately, the healing prescription she needed couldn't be purchased with the latest Kate Spade bag or Christian Louboutin heels. The Walgreens rewards card wouldn't help either. It couldn't be borrowed or exchanged no matter the item capable of being bargained. Craigslist couldn't sell it and Fisher-Price couldn't manufacture it.

Before the enemy tries to convince you of the similarities between the healing Jennifer needed and the watered down healing you've believed God for, let me make this clear. This is not referencing diluted healing where you're good as long as "they" don't bother you, text you, post Facebook statuses indirectly, or sit near you at church. It's not about this tainted healing where you avoid certain popular places to ensure you don't run into one another. No ma'am, no sir. Buckle up and brace yourself. This is in reference to total healing that comes from God and God alone. Healing that embodies the truth that no matter what they do or say, even how they act, you are FREE. They can come for you on any given day but your mind has been programmed and fixed to visualize the table God is preparing for you right before their very eyes. Let's talk about freedom for a moment, shall we?

Jennifer wasn't the average girl. She was a faithful churchgoer, listened to sermons from the world's most popular pastors almost daily, and had a prayer life that existed, though not always consistent. She kept current with the most viral sermon through the podcast app on her smart phone. She knew when God was speaking for the most part and accepted the idea behind Him speaking in unorthodox ways. She could recite the ever so famous scriptures concerning forgiveness and how men and women ought to forgive so that our Father in Heaven forgives us. She heard about the importance of going to those who had offended you and getting it right so that her prayers could be heard. Yep, all of that she knew and knew well. Yet and still, she kept a track record of all those who offended her over the years. Their names were written in pen, as intentions of ever erasing them didn't exist. To be honest, there were a few individuals who couldn't afford another tally mark before being completely dismissed from her life and thoughts. Let's not even discuss those who had sadly made some of the same mistakes twice. They are lucky to have any access to her at all. This was her way of dealing with offense. Well, not dealing with it, shall we say? Jennifer had a huge heart and always examined her choices prior to making them to ensure the other party would not feel offended or open a door to have any malice in their heart toward her following the decision made. She hated confrontation or misconstrued feelings more than anything.

One cold, foggy winter morning, Jennifer stumbled across a podcast from one of her favorite world trailblazers in ministry titled, "Nothing Just Happens." Based on the title alone, she knew some stirring would take place once the segment ended. The Bishop formed his message based on the theory that nothing happens by accident. Every event in our lives have purpose and will ultimately work for the good of those who love God and are called according to His purpose. (Romans 8:28). He tells of the story of a woman named Naomi whose husband passed away. Everything in life is orchestrated so that we understand there is some master plan at work in which we typically cannot see with our natural eyes. Ruth's mother in law endured several terrible experiences of losing her husband, companion, and longtime lover as well as her two sons. One daughter in law decided to cling to Naomi and vowed to stay with her and that Naomi's God and people would be her God and people. Ruth decided to go into the fields to pick up leftover grains. We later see that she worked behind the harvesters in a field, which belonged to a man named Boaz. Boaz kindly informed Ruth she could work safely in his fields and get a drink when she felt thirsty. At the time, Ruth didn't know Boaz had heard of Ruth's kindness toward her mother in law and that the Lord would surely bless and reward her for doing so. In the end, Boaz acquires the land, which belonged to Naomi, and eventually marries Ruth.

The story may have turned out much differently had Ruth remained sorrowful after her husband's death. She could have become bitter and never received the double portion of blessings Boaz bestowed upon her. She could have stayed in Moab and never witnessed the good, which came after a horrible season in her life. It was a season that would have caused many to be angry with God for an extensive period of time. Jennifer thought back on her own history and judged how she reacted rather than responding to circumstances that could have possibly changed the course of her life for the better had she done so.

When God closes a door, there is no need in trying to shake the lock. It's best to let the door close as God knows better than we do. Once He blocks it, there's no point in stalking it. The pastor moves across the pulpit shouting and encouraging his members to let people go. Release them out of your spirit and out of your mind. Clearly this was easier said than done, Jennifer thought. He then goes on to say that we keep looking at the puppet on the stage. But God is trying to get us to see the master behind the curtain. In a puppet show, everything has strings on it. The real artist is the puppet master who's moving strings and puppets sometimes simultaneously. This is their job that they've learned and mastered to perfection. In essence, God has a string on everything in our lives. Many people walked away from us because they were merely props. When they completed the task they were purposed to do, God snatched them out. God is moving us systematically toward a predestined end. Our mess-ups are setups.

By this time, the small amount of makeup Jennifer had applied to her face was slowly fading away as tears raced down her cheeks uncontrollably. She had never heard someone's escape put into words in this manner before. She rehearsed in her mind several individuals who were no longer apart of her life. Some she thought for sure would be with her 'til the rocking chairs. Ironically, Jennifer never saw any of the individuals she thought of in public places. Not the mall, dollar store, Target, or even a gas station. It was almost as though once their segment of her show ended, they were erased from the face of the earth. Deleted from the cast members' section of the credits. They served their ultimate purpose and that was that. Unfortunately, Jennifer never allowed herself to come to terms with what was ultimately a God move. More often than not, she took everything personal. She thought of the many times she was there for them and would come to their beck and call at the drop of a dime. She thought of events in her life that had yet to take place that she never once doubted their presence once those special events took place. She thought back specifically of being engaged to her first love, or childhood friends whom she eventually parted ways with as they got older for various reasons.

She felt her heart beginning to hurt at just the thought of them, as though she was reliving the exact moment they walked out of her life. Their departure wasn't the type for either of them to try and find her years later or search on Facebook. It was the end. Ride or die was the only type of attribute she cared to possess when it came to friends and relationships. Jennifer held all relationships on a pedestal as genuine; friendships were hard to come by. For her, it may not have been the fact that "they" had to leave her and the chapter in her book called life, but it was the way in which they left. Their leaving came across as though it wasn't of importance, and that they could find another Jennifer anywhere. She was replaceable, and that's just life.

Jennifer always enjoyed traveling and enjoyed popular tourist attractions in other areas. Flying was always more relaxing than traveling by car to any destination longer than five hours. She was no stranger to flying but somehow always managed to pack something in her carry-on bag that was too big according to TSA's recommended list. By this point you would think she had the prohibited items list memorized. More than a time or two she was forced to throw away some of her most favorite scented hand lotions. Certain items such as an umbrella, child restraint seats, and food or drinks purchased after clearing the security checkpoint were permitted. Depending on the airline, one or two carry-on bags maximum were accepted at no charge. No maximum weight applies to carry-on bags except in certain stations. One day, God had a perfect way of revealing to her the perfect analogy as it related to what she wanted to carry-on with her on this flight to destination. Just as airlines and TSA have put stipulations in place as to what can or cannot go on an airplane, so has God with what can accompany us to our destination called destiny. Of course Jennifer knew that even certain firearms and ammunition weren't allowed on a plane unless it's locked and transported as checked baggage.

In that moment, she realized that bitterness was prohibited for the journey to which God had called her to travel. No way around it. It couldn't be checked in no matter the dire need the passenger may think they have of it. On the contrary, there are many other items that can go with no reservation. Those things are love, happiness, joy, peace, hope, faith, and so much more. When was the last time you checked your baggage before you left home? Have you too been stopped at checkpoint and forced to throw something out, as it wasn't allowed to go?

God: 1, Me: 0

For my thoughts are not your thoughts, neither are your ways my ways, saith the LORD. For as the heavens are higher than the earth, so are my ways higher than your ways, and my thoughts than your thoughts. (Isaiah 55:8-9)(KJV)

The steps of a good man are ordered by the LORD: and he delighteth in his way. (Psalm 37:23)(KJV)

I will go before thee, and make the crooked places straight. (Isaiah 45:2)(KJV)

"If I give it to you NOW, you'll only abuse it. I'm not moved by giving you something just because others around you seem to hold the promise. That's not how I operate."

"But you promised to give me beauty for ashes, oil of joy instead of mourning, and a garment of praise for a spirit of heaviness," she mumbled under her voice. "How can you be such an infinite, sovereign, and absolute God that millions worship and yet not deliver on Your promises? Or drag Your feet for that matter? Isn't that a little misleading? The ability to change my circumstances in a matter of seconds is at Your fingertips. But You avoid me and my cries daily. All power is in Your hands, remember? I'm sick of hearing how much of an on-time God you are when you seem to be on CP time concerning my destiny."

I'm not referring to the CP time where you arrive at church during praise and worship. Nah. I'm speaking of the CP time where the pastor has everyone slain in the spirit and can barely give the benediction. The CP time where all the hot fish at the family reunion is nonexistent and not a cold can soda left in sight, not even at the very bottom of the cooler. God and I clearly had a love/hate relationship most days.

"There are times when I visualize You sitting on a red, distorted bench with one leg crossed, a cup of 7/11 coffee in one hand, tapping Your feet, and reading a book at Your leisure. Basically, not a care in the world. If You would have never told me about the promise, I wouldn't be in a position of anticipating it as much as I do. Couldn't You have kept that a secret since the season in which You spoke it was growing longer by the day? Why aren't spiritual seasons congruent with natural seasons anyway? I yearn for it like medicine to a sick child or whiskey to an alcoholic. But since You released those words, it's my only desire to have it and have it now. I daydream about it daily without realizing. In fact, my daughter catches me smiling while driving as she focuses on my rear-view mirror. I giggle and with excitement tell her about the vision, which has me so giddy. Why must You sit in Heaven and watch me weep in hopes of attaining the unknown? Don't You know how bad it hurts to sit and wait? All our lives consist of waiting for the next whatever to happen. Be not weary in well doing doesn't apply to me."

Ashley assumed she could gently nudge God into changing His mind and releasing His promises if she whined a certain way. He cared for her indeed, but not enough to watch while she self-destructs herself with something she wasn't prepared for. It wasn't enough for her to sit and watch others obtain the very things God had promised her. Like Jacob, she wrestled with God, not fully comprehending it was a lost cause. But one thing's for sure, and two things for certain, she wasn't letting go until He blessed her. At times, God only releases His blessings on us after a period of extended and even painful wrestling with Him. Though Jacob wrestled with God, it was God who ended the fight. He dislocates Jacob's hip and calls for absolution. There was no way she was leaving the earth without seeing a manifestation of all that He had promised. It wasn't long ago that God had given her a glimpse of the promise. Ashley had rented an apartment for a few years. After seeing her mother purchase a home, she started to desire a home as well. For years she refused to even consider home buying until she was married. Ashley was very traditional and wanted to share such an experience with the love of her life. But each year she renewed her lease, the leasing company increased the rent. So, she knew it was time to make a move. From then on she was determined to become a homebuyer by the age of twenty-five. She went through the necessary mechanics of having her credit restored, and then working with a realtor. He encouraged her to build a home from the ground up which Ashley couldn't help but be excited and anxious about. She was able to pick out cabinet and shutter colors, carpet type, and even the floor plan of the home. Once they broke ground, Ashley couldn't help but drive by her soon to be home two to three times a day. In the midst of this happening, Ashley was never motivated enough to start packing boxes.

After a while, issue after issue seemed to arise which made the process extremely stressful and less exciting. Every time the underwriters requested something and she fulfilled the request, another request was made. After the home was built, something strange happened. One night, Ashley was awakened by the voice of God. Very clearly He informed her that she was accepting something He never designed her to accept. Those were His only words. The next morning, Ashley quickly phoned her grandmother to find out what this meant as she always seemed to have wisdom on most situations. Her grandmother told her that whatever it was she didn't need to accept, and Ashley already knew deep down what it was in reference to. Immediately, she came to terms with this revelation being about the home. Deep down Ashley wanted so much more. But as a single parent the enemy had certainly forced her mind to believing a bigger home wasn't possible given various circumstances. That day she informed her realtor she didn't wish to move forward with the process. He had no hesitations in telling her she was making a huge mistake. At that moment, Ashley only wanted what God wanted for her, and that was His best without settling.

That day she experienced such a peace after making a hard decision. It was a tough decision many didn't understand and questioned if she really heard from God. God said 'no' and Ashley was forced to come to terms quickly with the fact that her agenda and timeline wasn't always His. What she didn't realize then was sometimes you have to lose to win again, and a major win was certainly soon to come. More times than not, she didn't pray fervently because she didn't want to face the 'no' that could come once her requests were made to God. In her mind no matter what she asked for, the answer would always be 'no,' as if He never wanted to see His daughter genuinely happy. Although He knew her better than she knew herself, she tried to convince her mind to believing there were some things she could actually hide from the Father. Truth is, there were blessings God wanted to put in her hands, but she wasn't mature enough to receive them. She had one thing in mind, but He had a better plan that would be marked more exceedingly, abundantly, above all than she could ever ask or think.

911! Hello?

Above all else, guard your heart, for everything you do flows from it. (Proverbs 4:23)(NIV)

Create in me a clean heart, O God,
And renew a right and steadfast spirit within me. (Psalm 51:10)(NIV)

The coronary artery has no longer brought blood to your heart. A blood clot has formed and obstructed your blood flow. Your heart has now become starved of oxygen-rich blood, and your nervous system has immediately sent signals to your brain about what's going on. By now, you're sweating and your heart rate has sped up. You may even be nauseous or weak at this point. Your nervous system has done its job and sent signals to your spinal cord and other parts of your body have begun to ache. Now, you've felt an immense chest pain that slowly crawled to your neck, jaw, ears, arms, wrists, shoulder blades, back, and even in your abdomen. You are having a heart attack.

He doesn't care. I'm convinced.
Does God have feelings?

Carest thou not that I am lonely? Carest thou not that I've been suffering more than a while? Carest thou not that they betrayed me when they promised they would be here forever? My ride-or-die. Well they died before the riding ever took place. Carest thou not that this isn't fair? Carest thou not that I stuck by their side and never told their deepest, darkest secrets to a soul? I mean the secrets that would destroy their reputation and bury them alive if plastered on the front of the local newspaper. Better yet a screenshot on everyone's social media feed. Yet and still, they walked off and left me for dead. Not only did they walk off, but they did it with such ease as if it was planned with great detail and strategy. Carest thou not that I've been faithful to the ministry when I needed a healing myself? Days I prayed for others when I stood in need of prayer myself.

"Lord, if You really love me, why do You allow such bad things to happen to me?" I cried, one warm, summer evening. The only thing being tested was my faith and patience in God. The only thing passing was a small strand of hope. How is it possible for a God so powerful and sovereign to not show compassion concerning the valleys I'm thrown in without warning? Or is it pity that

I'm after? Nope, that's not it at all. I've heard the saints say that God cares for us even more than we care for our own children. Is that even true? All things considered, if a child is in need of a Band-Aid, an antiseptic cloth, or a cast for that broken arm, a real mother is going to be sure that her child is well taken care of. She takes pride in being the nurturer and will drop any and everything at any given moment to come see about her baby. Strangely enough, it doesn't seem as though God comes to my rescue when I need Him most. If and when He does, it usually seems to be too late. I'm on the very cusp of not even believing there is a God and You drag Your feet concerning my healing that I so desperately need? Why are You not concerned about that which concerns me, God? I've suffered for more than a while, sir. This famine of love, famine of dis-ease, and famine of brokenness taunts me night and day.

Though not in a mood to read any type of scripture reference, I calmed myself down long enough to plop on my bed and open my Bible. Normally, the app on my iPhone was the go-to. But today, I needed to feel the word physically, spiritually, and emotionally. Rather than focusing on a particular scripture, or glancing at my Bible concordance, I allowed the Holy Spirit to lead me to the text I needed at that given moment. To my surprise, I landed on the text in Genesis concerning Joseph and the events leading up to him being thrown in the pit and thereafter. For a second, I couldn't believe what I was seeing. This must be make-believe, I thought. According to the text, Joseph was a teenage boy envied by his other brothers. Since he was the eleventh son of his father Jacob, one can expect sibling rivalry happening nonstop. Joseph was openly loved by his father and such favoritism was certainly envied by his brothers. To make matters worse, Jacob presented Joseph with a highly decorated coat. Shortly after, Joseph decides to relate his prophetic visions with his family, which showed that he would one day rule over his family. Of course animosity intensified and now his siblings wished to kill him. Instead, they sell him as a slave and deceive their father into thinking his favorite son had been slain by wild beasts.

Though this is the Bible, and even sounds a little unbelievable, many individuals have faced similar family issues. Joseph was sold to a high-ranking Egyptian named Potiphar. Despite the unfortunate circumstances, Joseph excelled at his duties and became one of his supervisor's most trusted servants, which led to him being in charge of the household. He was certainly a favored man. Things were going well for him, which meant something of the opposite was clearly on the horizon. Potiphar's wife was more than impressed with Joseph's doings and decided to attempt to seduce him. Sadly, her efforts were opposed. One can imagine her embarrassment, which led to her falsely accusing him of attempted rape. Joseph was innocent but his word against hers must not have turned out in his favor since he was cast into prison.

It's funny how even bad things can have purpose and work for our good. In the end, Joseph is made a ruler in Egypt, second only to the king. A famine strikes just as Joseph saw in his dreams. Oddly enough, his father sends ten of his sons to Egypt to buy grain. While there, the ten sons meet their long-lost brother. It was the same brother they sold as a slave. At this point Joseph was unrecognizable. They bow down to him, fulfilling a previous prophecy Joseph told. Afterwards, Joseph reveals his identity and forgives their wrongdoing immediately. By this time, my eyes are watery as I tries to understand what took place. After every adversity Joseph faced, His heart stayed pure. In my eyes I never believed such a thing was possible. His circumstances were very much unjust, but he remained faithful understanding that God knew and saw all. Most people would have applauded Joseph if he had turned his brothers away knowing they were in need.

On this day, I learned the significance of God's sovereignty to overcome evil and bring me into His perfect plan with ease. After all his trials, Joseph could clearly see God's hand and power at work in his life. Later, Joseph reassures his brothers, speaking with them heart-to-heart, offering forgiveness, and saying, "You intended to harm me, but God intended it for GOOD." At that moment, everything "they" did seemed so little and insignificant in comparison to how God sees it all. My future wasn't predicated on that which was. Before then, when I was in pain, the first thing the devil did was tell me, "God doesn't even care." He was such a liar, and a good one at that. Nevertheless, I found myself encouraged. I felt vindicated whether they ever got what they deserved or not. In the end, God was still going to prosper me according to His perfect plan. Matters of the heart can only be resolved with the help and guidance of the Maker of the heart. The symptoms of having a heart attack slowly faded away. If anything, as long as I kept my heart right, showed mercy, and extended forgiveness, everything was well. And yes, even when it didn't "seem" well. I no longer had to rack my brain wondering how, when, and how God was going to justify me. I trusted Him. And ultimately, He would never leave nor forsake me. He would protect His daughter at all costs.

A small smile spread across my face. Days of bleeding internally and crying silently for help because of my bitterness were now of the past. In the palm of His hands, there I was. God loved me and no one or nothing could stop that love from permeating.

Heart attacks are the number one cause of death in many parts of the world. It's obvious that we need to pay careful attention to what the medical professional is saying about heart attack prevention. He clearly instructs us to "guard your heart above all else." Our heart represents a dwelling place where our feelings, attitudes, words, and actions are conceived. Christ makes His home in our hearts and it's where His Spirit dwells. It is in our hearts that we receive from God. So if anything, our hearts cannot afford to collect anything that's disruptive to our physical and spiritual health. Perhaps you too need a bulletproof vest to protect your heart from possible danger. Keeping your heart healthy undeniably makes your life more enjoyable and fruitful. God's desire is for us to have a healthy natural heart as well as a healthy spiritual heart. You have a race to run in this thing called life. Be sure to protect your heart so you can avoid a heart attack and keep your cardiovascular system performing at its best. It's safe to say false alarm now.*

Miranda's Rights

There is a way which seems right to a man and appears straight before him, But its end is the way of death. (Proverbs 14:12)(AMP)

"You have a right to not remain bitter. Anything you say or hold with a tight grip can and will be used against you in the court of healing and wholeness. You have a right to an altar and access straight to Heaven. If you cannot afford an altar, I suggest you kneel down and create one right where your feet stand or possibly phone a friend. Do you understand the rights I have just read to you? With these rights in mind, do you wish to confess there is an issue, which calls for surgery of the heart?"

The officer's stern military voice and intimidating, tall, masculine frame blinded her ability to focus. Though her rights were read and she understood the officer loud and clear, she still felt as though she may need to ask him to repeat himself. After a quick glance she decided maybe that wasn't such a good idea. In her mind, she had a right to harvest everything in her heart that held her captive of a life of freedom. Those who hurt her could have chosen another alternative. Even the few who left could have stuck it out with her. So she believed. Captive. Yes, that's one word that described her perfectly. She knew in her Bible somewhere of a scripture that referred to liberty in God's presence. But that was just something she read; it was nothing of what she believed. She recalled a scripture a pastor read while flipping through channels one Sunday afternoon. It read: "They left us, but they were never really with us. If they had been, they would have stuck it out with us, loyal to the end. In leaving, they showed their true colors, and showed they never did belong."

Was it true they never belonged? If they didn't, why did God even allow their paths to cross? Surely he could have blocked the initial contact. Her child's father didn't have to leave. His flesh didn't have to desire other women. He ruined her plans of telling their children he was her first and last. Most men would kill to date a woman they had the pleasure of being the only one she was ever intimate with. She wasn't bad looking, always easy on the eyes, and was a Christian woman. New Year's Eve night you could always find her at someone's church. She even served in a few ministries at her local church. Did I mention she was a tither? Her hair was a beautiful, healthy length combined with a pretty curvy figure. Men gathered in her inbox immediately after posting a beautiful selfie that highlighted her radiant beauty free of any filters. Surely those ingredients together made a fit wife. She was more than enough to be the woman he needed. Truth is, she expected a pint man to love her on a gallon level. For years, she tried to revive that which was dead. Prayer after prayer pleading with God to make him desire her the way she wished so their child could grow up in a two-parent home. That's all she ever wished for. She never wanted her daughter to live a life through friends who had two parents in the home because she knew what that felt like.

All she hoped for was both parents to attend parent/teacher conference, family vacations together, and family dinners each night at the dining room table. Her father didn't have to live his life as though she never existed. Yes, he went away for eight years. But that time could have been redeemed had he desired a genuine relationship with her. He wasn't forced to carry himself like a child. That was by choice. An apology would have been nice. She didn't expect him to be perfect but to at least put forth an effort, and a minimal one if anything. Surely, this wasn't too hard for a BIG God to accomplish, and honestly, she believed this prayer wasn't asking too much either. The tears she'd cried many days distorted her vision of seeing this as a God thing and had nothing to do with her value or self-worth. Bitterness crept in and tainted her ability to trust. "I've sown love so why am I reaping rejection?" she constantly asked herself. There is a love so grand, so wide, and so deep that will one day consume her until she can barely stand it.

Healing had received her, but she hadn't received it. She hadn't disassociated pain with the gender. You see, Miranda had experienced a great deal of blessings if you will. A trickle here and a stream there. But nothing compared to the flood God wished to send without warning. There was a land flowing with milk and honey He patiently waited for her to tap into. The nourishment and the sweet stuff. Knowing this, she still chose to walk around with her arms in handcuffs as though freedom was never her birthright. She was only guilty of the crime by choice, not by actual deed.

You know Miranda Rights to be a right to silence, and a warning given by police in the United States to suspects in police custody. Anyone in police custody must be told the four things before being questioned. The officer must ensure the suspect understands his or her rights. It is significant to note that Miranda Rights do not go into effect until after an arrest is made. Similarly, you've been in custody a time or two as well. Bitterness zipped your lips shortly after your arrest and ultimately kept you from reaching your higher purpose.

Truth is, I gave up all rights when I gave my life to Christ. I am dead. My flesh is dead. Therefore, I have no rights to hold onto anything not like Christ. His spirit moves and dwells in me as I am a product of Him.

Consider yourself Mirandized.

Room 143

Hatred stirreth up strifes: but love covereth all sins.
(Proverbs 10:12)(KJV)

Hate what is evil; cling to what is good. (Romans 12:9b)(NIV)

Love does not dishonor others, it is not self-seeking, it is not easily angered, it keeps no record of wrongs. Love does not delight in evil but rejoices with the truth. (I Corinthians 13:5-6)(NIV)

Do you want to be healed? This is the first question one must ask themselves on the road to healing. I had to admit to myself that I was sick and tired of being used by bitterness. I was sick of the side effects this drug had done to me. I had played with that overly used bandage long enough. Even a handy First-Aid kit wouldn't do the trick for the transformation I so greatly needed in my life. Honesty is always the first step. In Luke 18:40, Jesus asked, "What do you want me to do for you?" I'm begging You; reveal your heart on today. I'm petitioning you to go to the throne, lie on your face, cry off that new MAC foundation and make your requests known to Him who knows all. Tell God this cancer can no longer rule in your life. Begin to pray concerning those circumstances that once embittered you.

In all honesty, this is the moment in which God has waited with open arms for you to come running like that of a three-year-old little girl whose father just returned from a two-week work trip. Fortunately, He is the ultimate healer yet He's been patient enough while you ran to friends and family members looking for advice on healing that only He could bring. He IS a big enough God to perform the surgery, change clothes, and comfort you following the procedure. I'm talking about the patience of God.

I asked my father in Heaven to remove "it" from "me". There were many days I felt as though I could hold on to the bitterness, the offense, the hurt, and the pain better than God could hold on and release my healing. My grip on this cancer seemed more powerful than His release of healing. So the enemy wanted me to think. Lord, show me what I'm forfeiting by holding on to this dis-ease. Prove to me why it's better to lay aside this weight that so easily entangles me. "Consider it done," he said to Himself without letting me in on His plans. The very next week, a very sharp businesswoman sowed two thousand dollars in my life within hours. Being the God that He is, of course,

He didn't stop there. I also received a MacBook Air from a childhood friend as a gift to finally get going on my first novel. I chuckled under my breath just before going to bed that night. "Lord, I guess You showed and proved, huh? You did it again, BIG guy."

I could visibly see Him flex His muscles that day, as if He had anything to prove to little ol' me. One thing for certain and two things for sure, He loves me, and guess what? He loves you just as much. How do I know that? Because His word tells us He is no respecter of persons. What He makes happen for one, He's more than able to make happen for another. So, if it's healing that you really want, I dare you to be bold enough and ask Him for it. I'm reminded of John 5:6 which says, *"When Jesus saw him lying there and learned that he had been in this condition for a long time, he asked him, 'Do you want to get well?' Another version asks, 'Do you want to be cured? Will you be made whole?'"* This text tells me that God won't force the healing on me, but He considers my wishes. He will not force-feed me medicine that He and I both know is detrimental to my healing.

Behind this question, I also assume that God knows He has the power to make me whole again but just needs me to confirm it. In other words, 'I have what you need and I'm ready as soon as you give me the okay to proceed.' That's good news. I can remember as a child, there were times I asked my mother for something not knowing if she had the power, means, or resources to carry it out. Isn't it comforting, knowing there's nothing too big, too wide, and too strong enough for our God to do? Ever know what it's like to ask something in confidence and have not a doubt in your mind that it's possible? You don't need a tarot card reading or another two-hour pillow talk session with your bestie. You don't need another confirmation or online assessment. What you need is waiting for you to acknowledge that you have need of it. I need you to want this more than you've ever wanted anything else in life.

Did you know that it warms God's heart when we have need of Him and ask Him for help? God will bring healing and hope out of your brokenness. He promised to give you beauty for ashes. I know you didn't expect this, but I have a favor to ask of you. Right now, grab a piece of paper or sticky note. I don't care if it's an empty gum wrapper. I want you to write down what's holding you back from being whole again. Before you write the names of those who caused you pain, grief, temporary inconveniences and therefore forced you into a prison jail, I want you to be honest with YOU. Blame will always keep the wounds open. Only forgiveness heals, according to Thomas S. Monson. Without bursting out, "You don't know what they did to me," force your pen to the paper and write. You've been operating with lack and getting by. But it's time for holistic living. It's time to live from a place of freedom. The world needs the greatest version of you. I'm convinced that someone's deliverance is tied up in your wholeness. Don't delay them any longer.

Imagine a midget just shy of three feet breaking into your home in mid daylight forcing you to give up all of your most prized possessions within minutes or he was going to kill you. Note that he didn't have a gun, not even a knife or a baseball bat. Just his bare hands. Your significant other or masculine type person present was the least of his worries. Oh, and the small triangular sign with ADT printed in large font didn't faze him much either. He stood in position like that of Muhammad Ali, sure of his intentions, and ready to get everything you've worked years for. Some of you, even decades. He was actually brave enough to knock first and then picked the lock when you didn't answer as soon as he preferred. Before he could finish his demand of your belongings, you ask him to hold for a moment as you walk upstairs to your safe and grab what he's after. As soon as you hit the fourth step, you heard his high-pitch voice began rattling off other items of his liking as he walked around the family room. Yes, he walked around marking his territory and would almost dare anyone else to do anything about it. He knew exactly what he came for and wasn't leaving until he came and conquered ALL. And just like that, you did what he asked with not an ounce of fight in you. His size was never life threatening to say the least.

The appointment is over, your insurance (faith) has been filed, and now it's time to check out. As mentioned at check-in, a co-pay in the amount of an open heart/mind has been taken care of. The doctor has ordered healing over the next however many days, months, years needed. I urge you to not prolong the specific orders per doctors' request. Dr. Jehovah-Rapha has ordered a prescription of confession, forgiveness, and faith to believe that you can be whole again. You shall take this medicine morning, noon, and night and any time in between when you feel the effects of this disease brewing again. The prescription has already been called into the pharmacy and you should begin the first dosage as soon as possible if you're looking to be whole again. Before you doubt his recommendations, I pray that you'll ask God to help your unbelief. Dr. Jehovah-Rapha has been in the business for many years and always knows just what the patient needs. In like manner, you're unable to change the flavor to grape or berry, I can assure you after a while, the taste gets more desiring and you'll find yourself not needing any artificially added flavors. Taking before or after a meal is not necessary either. The doctor prefers that even on an empty stomach, you do not forfeit the ability of healing and the power of being freed. Side effects may include but are not limited to a new you emerging, stomach cramps, new vision, and a healthy heart free of any clogged arteries. Please note that you can up the dosage at any time. Before starting the medications, Dr. Jehovah-Rapha has recommended a catheter to flush out all parts of your flesh that may want to hinder this transition.

I pray that God's love pierces through your heart sharper than anything you've ever witnessed. So much so that you don't have to question is such a thing even possible. To the point where you feel it running through your veins and it stirs up something within the pit of your belly. No more wrestling, no more doubting, no more faking, and no more masks. Surrender all today. Take off your wounds, grab the hospital nightgown, and prepare for surgery. Decide to no longer hold yourself back. I promise to hold your hand until recovery. Walk in your healing. Walk in your freedom. Walk in your wholeness. You don't have to stay in the shape that you're in. Because the potter wants to put you back together again. He loves you. More than you will ever know or comprehend.

Stand Up to It!

I can do all things [which He has called me to do] through Him who strengthens and empowers me [to fulfill His purpose—I am self-sufficient in Christ's sufficiency; I am ready for anything and equal to anything through Him who infuses me with inner strength and confident peace.](Philippians 4:13)(AMP)

He gives strength to the weary,
And to him who has no might He increases power. (Isaiah 40:29)(AMP)

Fight or flight.

I take it you've suffered a while with this bully called Bitterness. The bully that made one clear their pockets for every dime of lunch money, leaving only pieces of lint behind. How does it feel to continuously be pushed and shoved around like a little punk? Ever wondered why a bully finally stopped attacking the victim? I can assure you it was because the victim took a stand and decided this is not how the story will end. It's time to talk for real. No more third person or numerous characters. No more storytelling and reminiscing. No sugarcoating. No hiding behind rocks. No blaming other people for why you feel the way you feel and hate the way you hate. No looking at memories in your news feed and feeling emotions you thought were six feet under. No time to phone a friend and have them agree with you about YOUR mess and throw shade on every individual involved. No talking to your pastor to have he or she speak to your true character and validate how good of a Christian you are. No pity-parties. Nope. None of that. This is you and I. You and "it".

The biggest misconception I've had about this thing called life was believing change was external rather than internal. Believing that I had every right to feel the way I did because of what "they" did even when nine times out of ten it was avoidable. It was believing that the nasty parts of me inwardly could not be seen externally so what's the point in changing? If God had forgiven me, then that's all I needed, right? Wrong! But what about His grace and mercy that's made new unto me each and every day? Daily, He loads me with benefits. I could always rely on that. Or what about this belief that the Lord knows my heart. His grace will cover me, right? Wrong. He is also a God of wrath and He does get tired, especially considering I know the right thing to do. Can I not get away with being bitter if God knew I had a desire to be a better person? He knows me better than I know myself. He is a patient God, you know?

I've ignored this truth for temporary happiness longer than necessary. Way too long. But now, I'm forced to face the reality. It's looking me dead in the eyes and I can't look away and pretend it's not there even if I tried. That reality is, I can't continue life with this disease, this burden, and this "thing" that's sucking the life out of me and affecting other areas of my life, including my ability to receive abundance, and my ability to be used by God. My ability to charter unchartered territory. My ability to go into places seemingly impossible. My destination of walking in His will for my life. This thing even has the potential to destruct my child and plant seeds in her that are sure to reap a harvest one day. I can't afford that. Not on my watch.

I refuse to affect her greatness because of my immaturity to deal with issues that have taken root and sprouted in my life over the years. She deserves more than that. I can't correct or undo what "they" did. But I can and will change how I let it affect my spirit. The spirit God dwells in and works to improve daily. It just isn't worth it. I have to be honest; I've masked this disease quite well over the years. Never had to see a specialist or go to a clinic. No antibiotics or medications administered. Masking it wasn't as bad as one would think. It wasn't something that was displayed over my face and visible to the eye. Oh no. It was far worse than sunburn or uneven eyebrows. The most expensive makeup couldn't conceal it and the best-rated dermatologist couldn't hide it even with the best procedure. Even cover girl can only cover so much. It was brewing and boiling in the pits of my stomach day in and day out. My God did I hide it well. I was active in my church, admired by many of my peers, and was even invited and chosen to speak and encourage youth.

You see, I've been blessed a great deal in my short time here on Earth. Many individuals would like to believe I had it made and success was given to me on a silver platter with a cluster of crab legs and buttered lemon sauce on the side. That's quite the opposite. One day, I eventually grew tired of changing masks to match each daily outfit. Talk about time consuming. It was tiring and defeating me like an individual suffering with stage four cancer. I couldn't take it anymore. The side effects had reared its ugly head and eventually ran its course in my life. I was tired of sprinkles of blessings here and there only to find myself back in the same stinky spot all over again just a few months later. God had an avalanche. Blessings that were sure to chase me down and eventually overtake me. A storm just like He gave Elijah when he prayed fervently and effectually. I deserved healing. My God sent His Word and died on the cross for me to walk in that healing, free of conviction. In all honesty, healing had already found me. But I wouldn't embrace it. Carrying my bitterness around like the latest handbag from the most upscale department store had become my norm. I was used to cuddling with "it" at night and I didn't like the idea of meeting fresh linen sheets hot out the dryer with just a pillow either. Far too long bitterness has robbed me of the greatest moments of life I could never even pay to get back. She stopped favor from favoring me. Countless times she invited herself into my home like a third wheel the day of prom. She greeted no one when she walked in the door and made herself comfy as though she'd been there dozens of times before.

Admittedly, I've dressed the part and gotten all glammed up with the best of them. My external appearance was everything and any given day I could be crowned "best dressed" for the class superlative. Though I was comfortable with my size, I was carrying something similar to a fifty-pound tumor on my heart. At any moment, it could kill me. It was the type of death that wasn't worth calling a paramedic for. I couldn't be revived. I was pronounced dead on the scene with no resuscitation. It appeared that I had mastered the art of killing myself softly.

As you're reading the words presented on these pages, I know many emotions and thoughts are circling your mind. You may even find your body temperature increasing. Out of all thoughts, I'm sure you're thinking "but you don't know what they did to me." You're probably wondering when vindication will take place. Restitution. Not realizing reciprocity doesn't exist when it comes to bitterness. They need to pay for what they did or didn't do plus more, right? Wrong again. The idea behind every page which formed this novel is to prove that whether they ever come to terms and apologize or at least feel some sort of remorse for what they did, or didn't do for a lack thereof, they don't owe you a thing. Ouch. As much as I heard those words prior to writing this novel, I could never seem to allow them to ease down my throat—even with a gallon water following. It just wasn't possible. Without thought, I spat that overly used statement out every single time I heard or read it. Let's pause for just a second and allow that to digest. Slowly, if need be. While you swallow that, I want you to think of another matter for a moment.

Recently, my mind began to wander and think of others who also walked around with such "infirmities" for many years. Immediately, the woman with the issue of blood came to mind. There was a woman in the Bible who had been subject to bleeding for twelve years. One can imagine this affliction was certainly an abnormal condition. She spent all she had and saw a great deal of many doctors but instead of getting better, she grew worse. Sort of like my bitterness. Medical treatment after medical treatment and still no sign of healing. This wasn't some headache or issue going on in her mind that could be cured with two pops of Advil or a thirty-minute session on some psychiatrist's couch. This was an affliction she could feel. I can only imagine how very desperate she was from dealing with such suffering. I'm quite positive at times she felt hopelessly incurable. Fortunately, there was a man who could heal her if only she could get to Him. She knew all about Him. She had seen Him perform healing miracles at the snap of a finger. Over and over she told herself, "If I could just touch His clothes, I'll be healed."

Let's pause for another moment here. There may be some eye rolling at this point, which is actually to be expected. Our natural eyes and disbelief prevent us from believing that touching someone's clothing will free us from bitterness. I get it. But at this moment, you aren't seeing with your natural eyes. You're seeing with your spiritual eyes. The prescription is expensive so stay focused. Only the pure in heart can see God. That's the only way you'll be able to receive and dissect what it is that's meant to come from this novel. Let's resume.

This unclean woman was not welcome in society. She was ceremonially unclean and restricted from touching a man in public. What's odd about this story is the fact that her illness did not prevent her from receiving what she so desperately needed. She was willing to break any and all social taboos. Nothing or no one else mattered at this point. Have you gotten fed up enough in your bitterness that you will go after healing no matter the cost? No matter the stirred up noses and staring eyes? No matter the indirect or direct posts on social media toward you? No matter what people who knew you back then will think of you?

More times than not, one needs to be circumcised from things that should have been cut away at birth. Then there are times when even after being circumcised, you have to go back and be cut again. Ouch. Look at the Israelites in the Bible. I had been carrying this deadweight around for over a decade that it never occurred I wasn't designed and created to live with it. It was sort of like a birthmark. I can only imagine how much this grieved God. Here He was, with all power in His hands and sovereign nature ready to give me access that would unlock so many things sure to break generational curses and cut the head of the oppressor wishing to hinder me from doing so. His hands were full with goodness but I blocked Him from releasing that to me. Isn't that insane? We block God from doing the very thing we're praying for Him to do because of our own self-inflicted wounds. If only we can get to a place where we are willing to let go of what's in our broken hands to receive what's in His mighty hands? Don't you want all that He has for you? Or have you grown comfortable in accepting the little?

For so long, I believed I could do a better job of holding on to the bitterness than God could do in releasing His goodness, as if I was on any level close to His. Tsk, tsk. It was my default mechanism and I didn't have another weapon that could do damage in an instant like holding on to this strong weapon could. How could I go into battle with nothing? What if I let "it" go and God didn't hold up His part of the bargain as He should? Then I'm left defeated and looking like such. I've heard Him to be not a man that He should lie, but that's all I did was "heard" about Him. After all, I had been waiting on many promises that had yet to come to fruition. I had my share of trusting men to do what they promised and when it came down to it, they never delivered, and without a single apology at that. My dad was notorious for that one. I wasn't about to let some God that I couldn't see and touch physically trick me into removing my grip only to back away and run with everything still in His hands. No way, no how. I wasn't going out like no punk. Truth is, I had been a coward all my life. I wouldn't stand up to "it". Like all dog owners say when you try to pet their "little" innocent pet at the park. "He's more afraid of you than you are of it." Yeah, right. I was no fool. But could this be true?

Ironically, God wanted to use me as a willing vessel, as a mouthpiece. He wanted to fill me up until I overflowed. His desire was to release that run over with His goodness type blessing. Full to the full. All along, the enemy had my mouth taped shut, daring me to speak against it to a single soul. I'm sure you could picture an aggressive male with his dirty, mechanic-looking hands gripped around a woman's neck daring her to move as he wished to violate her most sacred place. There is low-hanging fruit that I can't grab because bitterness had handcuffed my hands and said, "I triple dog dare you." It was one thing for me to confront "it" in my mind. I was bold there. Oh, yeah. Perhaps even scream out a curse word or two. In my mind, I took mess from no one and stood tall over-shadowing anyone that felt confident enough to step in my space. But there was no option of bringing "it" up to others without "it" putting me back in my proper place. Confined to an empty dark room behind bars. What if bitterness wanted to be cut from me like that spirally, disgusting looking umbilical cord attached to a newborn baby. Unfortunately, I was too stubborn and selfish to let go. Isn't that crazy? To continue holding on to something ultimately willing and ready to administer your last breath but you're holding on to "it" for dear life? "It" was ready to take me out without any help from an entourage. Meanwhile, I stood waiting for my girls to help me form an all-female gang to take "it" out.

As much as I stayed and wallowed in that mess, year after year, deep down I knew that once I became free, God was going to cause so many other women to get in formation and follow suit. He showed this to me in a clear vision one day. All over the world I was going from city-to-city, state-to-state, and country-to-country. The line of women following behind me grew exponentially. Scales were being removed from their eyes and chains were breaking at the drop of a dime. He was giving me influence and affluence over the masses. Something uncommon. My great grandmother probably prayed this prayer for her descendants' way before she ever saw their faces in the natural. Yet I was stuck on me, hindering their deliverance. How obnoxious and self-centered. I didn't mean to be this way. My heart just needed some work. I take that back. I didn't need a repaired or refurbished heart. I needed a new heart from one donor and one donor only. God. Besides, you cannot heal a wound without treating the source of the infection. Every time I tried to shake myself of this feeling, it only lasted a few days, and then I was back in the same rut that always had me bound. He desired to take me from the pit to the palace without a title, degree, or dollar value behind my name. My God was I sick and tired of being bound. Attending church every Sunday and Bible study each Wednesday. Bound. Watching sermons from the most prominent speakers while taking good notes. Bound. Posting spiritual and thought-provoking messages on social media by the hour. Still bound. Bound by bitterness. Everything that I said which looked appealing to one's eye was never bringing me any closer to my healing that I couldn't afford to live without at this point.

One day, a more seasoned woman who happened to sit on the pew in front of me every Sunday turned to ask me a question. She heard about me writing a book and wished to know the status of its completion. For some odd reason, she assumed I was married after looking at the title. I told her 'no,' curious as to why she asked. "What do you know about bitterness?" She questioned, as if bitterness discriminated according to age. In fact, bitterness didn't care one bit of when you were born.

As you have seen throughout the pages of this book, God's word and hearing it in my spirit over and over has helped a great deal. Somehow, when I thought a sermon title would discuss one subject, it ended up bringing up my bitterness at some point in the message. Within the first thirty seconds of the podcast Bishop Jakes mentioned a bitter person. Rather than exit out and find another audio to tune in to, I decided I wouldn't let "it" punk me down anymore and cause me to run and hide. The message opens discussing how the temporary frustration of waiting for something to come to fruition often causes one to become bitter. Because it didn't happen when we wanted it to, doesn't mean it's not going to happen. But I've found this is when the enemy does His greatest work. He floods our minds with thoughts that God's love for us is contingent on how soon He comes or answers when we are in need of Him. I can't tell you how many times I've questioned the accuracy of His timing. Bishop Jakes goes on to provide an example in the word concerning Lazarus's death. Lazarus was dead and God seemed to have taken His precious time to get to him.

If you've lived a while, you can agree that sometimes God doesn't do what you think He should do, when you think He should do it, or even how you think He should. In fact, Mary told Jesus, "If You would have been here, my brother wouldn't have died." Sounds like a bitter woman, right? There was no 'thank you for coming,' or anything. Bishop Jakes goes on to discuss the truth that bitter people often blame you for their problem. When life doesn't turn out the way we think it should, we look for someone to blame rather than taking responsibility for our own actions. Sound familiar? Just because life has put you on pause doesn't mean it has stopped you all together, or that you'll never hit play again. That's exactly what the enemy wants you to believe is true. But faith tells us, it's quite the opposite. God will cause ALL things, not some, to work for the good of those who love Him and who are called according to His purpose. (Romans 8:28).

I love this next point Bishop states. Periodically, throughout your life you will hit turbulent places. That is a given. The Bible says it will rain on the just and the unjust. If you aren't careful, bitterness will creep into your life and you will take this as an indication that life is over. Look at the story of Naomi in the bible. Don't let life make you change your name. When you believe that because you had a series of losses life is now over, you have stepped into the spider webs of being bitter without even wishing to. Bitterness is developed when things on the outside have contaminated what's on the inside. By now, I'm sure you're wondering how someone is telling your story whom you've never met. It takes consistent, hard work to keep things on the outside from getting on the inside. It never comes easy and never will. A series of losses will affect how you see yourself, how you feel about life, and how you approach your future, says Bishop Jakes. On the outside, many of us look the part. But if there was a device that could scan us from the head down as officers do at many large events for security measurements, many are contaminated and the wand would beep or flash lights instantaneously. The majority of us are contaminated with great potential and even greater destinies. Millions of us have allowed our pasts to bleed into our present and pollute our futures far worse than pollen in our environment on a bad day. Sadly, we can see it in others and call them out before we admit we're carrying the same toxins, if not more. Until we call it what it is, freedom will never be ours. Once that small ounce of bitterness invades us, we tend to give up and become cynical.

For me personally, rather than risk hoping again, or getting hurt again, it was easier to put multiple people in one broad category. Here began the process of walls being built up in my heart. The Bible says to guard your heart, not prevent others from getting to you. Jakes then goes on to say that when you have bitterness down in you, it affects your judgement. If this isn't true, I don't know what is. As my level of bitterness increased year after year, I found myself judging certain situations or people inaccurately because I assumed the situation would play out as times past. Because of this effect on my internal eyesight, I wasn't able to see what God was doing in my life. What was tainted was my vision of what is and what is to come. How could I let something so miniscule have that much power over me? Wow. By now, I have definitely come down your pew and read your mail. Why didn't I realize then that falling out with people and holding grudges was keeping me from seeing straight? In the natural, I had always had 20/20 vision. But internally, I had vision like that of a blind woman needing a service dog.

We have to work at getting along with each other and with God. Otherwise you'll never get as much as a glimpse of God. Make sure no one gets left out of God's generosity. Keep a sharp eye out for weeds of bitter discontent. A thistle or two gone to seed can ruin a whole garden in no time. (Hebrews 12:14-15 MSG).

In other words, God is saying but for no other reason, keep your vision clear and try to get along with people so that you can survive and "see" what God is up to. One or two small disagreements can affect your entire harvest that God wishes for you to see manifested. Even now, you can look back on a series of events that took place in your past, whether it was in your childhood or adult life, and look how you handled certain situations that resulted in seeds of bitterness being planted. And now, there's a root. Leaves can blow away, but a root cannot. In fact, the leaves will even change colors. And you'll look up and still see the root planted firm. This root springs up and gets in your emotions forcing you to become troubled. Like myself, I'm sure you continue praying about the leaves. Praying that God will cause them to stop doing what it is they're doing that frustrates you so much. On the contrary, God is more concerned with the root, your heart. For out of the abundance of the heart, the mouth speaks. Out of your heart flow the issues of life. All your tongue is doing is telling what's in your heart. Furthermore, when you are bitter, you cannot trust your own judgment. You will tend to make bad decisions because of the spirit in which you're operating from. There is a place in you where bitterness is lodged in and the enemy uses it to spoil you and contaminate you when you think no one is looking.

After a while, I came to the realization that I didn't need a fix. I didn't need another prophecy or revelation from God. Not even another dream or vision. I didn't need a scripture tattooed on my body or results from a personality test. I had to be honest with God and call a spade a spade. I was a bitter woman. Yikes. Hearing myself say that out loud and typing it out makes me sad and happy at the same time. Sad I nurtured "it" for so many years. I mean I fed that thing well. Yet I was happy to finally be at a place of maturity where I can openly admit that with no shame or blame. I don't care who's watching or hears it. You'll see why shortly. I took it off. I didn't want to carry it with me anymore. Now that I was bold enough to call it by its name, we could move on to the next step. Perhaps you too have shied away from the reality of your situation way too long. Call it what it is. There's no point in skirting around it any longer. Maybe you need to open your mouth at this moment, and just call it what it is. Not in your head or under your breath either. If you're at work, take a quick break and run to the bathroom or bend under your desk. But you have to say it out of your mouth without mumbling.

I'm not saying shout it to the mountaintops, but be assertive in knowing that now, you're about to have "it" under your feet once and for all. Get excited. That should have been enough for a small smile to form at the corners of your lips. I'll even take a smirk at this point. Relax. It gets better. My granny always knew there was a spirit there unlike God. We had a very close relationship unlike most have with their grandparents. She was and still is my best friend. She called me out on it often with not a care in the world. I would always get defensive and pray the conversation turned rather quickly. In her years, she had seen what bitterness had the power to do to a believer. Not just as a pastor, but as a person striving to walk in righteousness as well. She refused to let the enemy run rapid in my life and rob me of the destiny God fashioned for me before I was ever a seed in my mother's womb. I am grateful to her for that.

One evening after work, I decided I couldn't hold this in any longer. If I could be honest and completely vulnerable with anyone, it was her. I hadn't prepared for a comeback if the conversation didn't go according to plan. It was what it was going to be at that point. I trembled to even get the words off my lips. My voice cracked and my fingers shook. I knew she wouldn't judge me. That was never a part of her nature. But I still felt like a naked girl in a room with a man ready to mistreat me. Remember, I hid this all my life, and very well might I add. Now it was time to remove the masks one by one. "Granny, I've been bitter for a long time now and I can't do this anymore. I'm frustrated and tired of living like this. I feel like every promise God has given me is being held up because this thing is still attached to me. Everything is postponed. My husband, my ideal career, and my freedom. I'm ready for God to release to me what is mine. That land flowing with milk and honey that I told you about before. I've reached the furthest destination I can go with it. I can't move from point A to point B right now if I tried. It's time for change." Like the good granny she is, there was no judgement on her end. I held my breath waiting for whatever was to come through the receiver. She was a woman that wouldn't sugarcoat a thing or stroke your ego when you were in the wrong. Even for her oldest grandchild. The opportunity to jump down my throat and condemn me never came. She simply commended me for being able to open my mouth and admit my infirmity.

I can remember a few years back God showing me a vision of a spiral staircase that led from my bed straight to Heaven. At the top, He sat with His head in His hands, waiting for me to awaken so that we could talk. He had watched me toss and turn all night. Recently I found scripture backing this vision of Jacob who had a similar dream. Angels were moving back and forth along that staircase. I understand that the angels hearken unto the voice of the Lord. In essence, when I speak, they are trained to take my words to God who in turn makes things happen.

One thing I can truly say about God is the fact that He will continuously reveal Himself "if" we desire to know more about Him. I recently came across a weekly email sent from the desk of Pastor Tony Evans. The email was titled *Preparing Hearts for Destiny* but I was a little shocked after reading the context of the article. Pastor Evans began discussing his annual visit to the doctor for a normal physical review that many of us are accustomed to. He explained that one particular part of the examination is called a stress test. His doctor puts him on a treadmill prior to a nurse attaching all sorts of wires and measurement devices to his chest. He is then asked to walk. While walking, the nurse or doctor increases the speed and incline. As I read the email I could visually see myself at the local gym and the fingers that dread adjusting the incline. I could deal with a little increase of speed but it was something about the combination of increased speed and incline that immediately forced my mind to think, "Why even bother?"

Pastor Evans goes on to explain the doctor's reasoning for the stress test is to analyze the conditions of his heart under various stressful situations. Though he could tell his doctor all day long that in his body he felt fine and his heart was in perfect condition, the chances of the doctor taking his word and not administering the test was pretty slim to none. In fact, I'm sure it's unethical in the health field to even consider such a thing. Pastor Evans brought out a good point, stating that we can read our Bibles, go to church, participate in edifying conversations, and all the while feel that our spiritual hearts are fine. We can wave our hands in the air, and even sing praises like everything is great. To be honest, we may even believe it ourselves. But God knows the true state of our heart and He will often allow a test to occur in order to produce an accurate diagnosis. I've learned in my times that even after I've failed many tests, He will retest me until I got it right. No matter how long it took. Talk about no child left behind. He is that type of God.

My granny would often ask why I even chose to go back around certain mountains after I'd seen the outcome from previous times. God wants us to know the truth about ourselves even when we try to disguise it to the best of our abilities. He wants us to see the good, the bad, and the ugly about who we are at our core. I've heard more times than I can count "the devil did this, and the devil did that." Pastor Evans speaks to this common notion by stating, "God will often allow adverse circumstances, even painful circumstances, in our lives as a test in order to reveal, strengthen, and develop our hearts for His destiny." I don't know about you, but I desire a healthy life. Even while reading this article, I was reminded of a popular scripture that says, "I wish above all things that thou mayest prosper and be in health, even as thy soul prospereth," (3 John 1:2). The fleshly part of myself doesn't always enjoy His ways, but I find peace in knowing that I serve a God who refuses to allow me to stink and rot in one area of my life but live happy and prosperous in another. Who I am as a whole concerns Him. Fortunately, He's never said this is the last time I'll put you back together. Guaranteed victory was on the other end of my bitterness. The more I gave up offense and grudges, the closer it came to me.

Let me explain it to you this way.

One day, God and I decided to take a *loooong* road trip. I spent the day before packing the best jumbo snacks and drinks. I had what seemed like dozens of outfits stretched out on the bed. Typical woman, right? I needed to over prepare just in case the weatherman was wrong. He was known to tell a fib from time to time. I packed maxi dresses as a provisional measure if the sun beamed just right and skinny jeans with a cute cardigan if the clouds wanted to come out and play. I even went out to the bedding store to get the most comfortable, fluffy pillows for what would be the trip of a lifetime. No games were being played about this road trip. We left out early the following morning to get a head start and beat the traffic for morning commuters heading to school and work. Fortunately, Pandora didn't have a cut on time because she was blasting as soon as we could put the car in reverse and head out the driveway. I had paid the extra four dollars and ninety-nine cents a month for no interrupted commercials so I could be the best passenger seat DJ known to man. He was the driver and I was responsible for refreshing the snacks and making sure we weren't getting tired of the latest hit stations. We both knew the lyrics to every song that came from the shuffle so our own little concert would have surely been a sold out show if we ever toured even the largest cities. We had a BLAST. Halfway there, He pulled over on the side of the road. I assumed we had a flat tire and it wasn't time for a restroom stop. He got out, walked over to the passenger side, and asked me to get out. He said we had come as far as we could come with the internal luggage I was carrying (bitterness). Though He wanted to finish the road trip together, He couldn't. I had to make a decision then and there or He would catch up with me on the other side.

I came across a social media post recently that said this: you either get bitter or you get better. It's that simple. You either take what has been dealt to you and allow it to make you a better person, or you allow it to tear you down. The choice does not belong to fate, it belongs to you. You and I both know_you've ducked and dodged this beast for far too long. Go to the enemy's camp and take back what he stole from you. It's time to stand up to it.

If you're anything like me, I wanted to find out what God said about my issues concerning bitterness rather than listening to the voices in my head. God had already affirmed and confirmed me so saying those affirmations aloud became a necessity.

***

❖ I release the need to embrace negative energy.

❖ I am whole.

❖ I am healed from all past hurt.

❖ I release bitterness and only attract love.

❖ Genuine relationships are looking for me everywhere I go.

❖ I release the desire to hold grudges.

❖ What "they" did doesn't and will not control who I am.

❖ My heart is pure and I make wise decisions to keep it healthy.

❖ My past does not and will not define who I am.

❖ I cut the cord between me and bitterness.

❖ I let go of the old so I might receive the new.

❖ What's coming is better than what's been.

❖ God will restore everything that was lost.

❖ I recognize the attack(s) are not personal but spiritual.

❖ I release the need to feel vindicated.

❖ God's promises for me are still yes and amen.

❖ Love lifted me and will continue to lift me.

❖ I trust God to perfect His perfect will for my life.

❖ I serve my past an eviction notice without warning.

❖ I am unapologetically FREE.

Pray this prayer, and pray in this manner:

Father, today I take the stand and acknowledge that I've held resentment and bitterness against

_____ longer than I ever should. I understand this small seed has now formed a root and I need Your help. I confess this as sin and ask You to forgive me. As I ask for forgiveness, I also forgive _____. Today, I release my grip on it so that I can receive Your goodness. I want to move forward and be all that you would have me to be. **Remind me, Lord, to not hold any more resentment, but rather to love this person. Father, I ask You to also forgive _____.**

Thank You for hearing and answering my prayer. In Jesus's name, Amen.

The Lord is not slow in keeping his promise, as some understand slowness. Instead he is patient with you... (2 Peter 3:9, NIV)

Cues Music

Per instructions of the will, embalming would not be necessary for this death. The church appeared to be crowded from the outside. Other visitors such as anger, wrath, hatred, and slander have all parked side by side directly in front of the large cathedral. They wouldn't miss their friend's death to save their lives. It was a dark, cloudy, rainy day contrary to the weatherman's predictions. Many of those attending had known "her" for years and couldn't fathom not having her around any longer. Who would they go to church with, dine at the finest restaurants, or gossip with now? Their lives had grown accustomed to having her around for decades.

With heads held low and handkerchiefs in pocket, each of them made their way up the few stairs and into the vestibule to pay their respects to one they would truly miss. Most of her friends and other relatives were ushered in to view the body and take their seats just prior to the family arriving. The organist played the finest tunes of "Missing You," while each attendee walked slowly and some even shaking in disbelief that this day was among them. In their minds, they reminisced on the good ole days of growing up, playing after school, school crushes, and high school proms.

Though no loud outbursts or close relatives making it a point to cause a scene for the attention they so dearly thirst for, there was one strikingly beautiful young lady over to the far right of the church who wept loudly to the point of others looking to match a face with the sudden cries. Ironically, she looked extremely similar to the woman lying in the coffin. Their facial features and body frame were nearly like that of identical twins. It was easy to note several individuals in the audience looking back and forth at the strong resemblance between the two.

This was the twentieth century, but it was nice to see every attendee respectful of the deceased and not attempt at taking any pictures since the service was conducted with an open coffin. In fact, not one individual as much as looked at their phone let alone try to videotape. Cell phones were put away and not so much as even a vibration from any notification was heard.

The eulogy was beautiful considering the occasion and who was being put to rest. Remarks from "her" pastor and childhood friend left more than a dozen individuals teary eyed resulting in sniffles and controllable sobs. An assortment of flowers stood on each side of the coffin, which were beautiful and fitting. Six pallbearers stood, two by two, and took their proper places ready to carry the cherry wood coffin to the exit doors. She carried her weight well and happened to be quite solid in nature. The paid musicians took cue and began playing the keys very faintly.

In Christian tradition, the funeral ends with a burial of the coffin in this case. Per usual, the funeral home had dug up a small section of dirt for the interment just about ten steps to the left of the exit doors of the church. Commonly, many individuals attending a funeral will leave following any closing remarks rather than heading to the gravesite. In the same light, many turned to head to their cars as only a handful walked toward the burial plot to silently say their final goodbyes. Women carrying all flowers from the house of worship nicely arranged them around the coffin. The service was very brief and music played from a relative's iPod for a few moments before the end of the service. There was no need at this point for any relatives or close loved ones to try and pry open the coffin again. This was the end and everyone had come to terms with that whether they liked it or not.

So on today, the coroner has already pronounced your bitterness dead. It has no more life. The funeral home is headed to your residence in the next half hour to come and collect the body. You may find yourself standing in disbelief of what took place as you watched "it" take its last breath. For many of you, you never witnessed death in this manner before but only read or heard about it. Since they're coming from across town, you have a few moments to take any last kisses and kindly get yourself together. Don't expect the members of the funeral home to have any unique sympathy because it's "you." This happens to be their job, which is performed daily, so don't be alarmed if one or all are coldblooded to this entire experience that's new for you.

Ultimately, she had to die. There's no question about it. In hindsight, you will look back at this day and no longer feel any remorse or regrets. You will celebrate this day. For it is this day that God allowed a new you to be birthed. A new you that has fought for years to get to this place of freedom free of any heaviness and blessing blockers. It's funny your mom told you even as a child not to associate with everyone wearing a smile, and to not speak to strangers. Not only did you welcome "her" in your circle, you shacked up with her for more nights than your calendar could remember. Walk to the kitchen. Grab your finest wine glasses. Then proceed to the refrigerator and grab the half empty bottle of Moscato resting on the refrigerator door. On the island kitchen you'll find a fat piece of chocolate cake. That's for you. Take a seat at the table and enjoy. Your life will never be the same again. Cheers.

Acknowledgements

I am eternally grateful for all the help and push I've received to write my first novel and birth a God-intended baby. I want to thank God for the opportunity to unapologetically share my past with countless others who struggle in this state. I am forever grateful for every revelation, download, and outpouring of His Spirit to complete such a grand task He started in me. To my family, friends, and midwives (you know who you are), thank you immensely for your love, prayers, and support as I pursue my father's business. I wouldn't be where I am without any of you.

About the Author

Brittany Jenkins is a take charge, creative businesswoman, writer, and speaker. She holds a Bachelor of Arts degree in Business from Belmont Abbey College. Brittany currently works as an investment professional where she has obtained her Series 7 and 63 financial securities licenses.

As a millennial, one of Brittany's divine assignments before reaching her heavenly destination is to lead by example and show women of all ages and backgrounds the importance of living a purpose driven life while shattering every glass ceiling known to man. She's called to be a modern day Elizabeth as she aids other women in walking in their essence of *Queendom.* As a single mother, Brittany is determined to encourage others that anything is possible when you trust God and have F A I T H. Even if you have to do so blindly.

When she is not pursuing her career endeavors, Brittany enjoys listening to music, traveling, and spending time with her daughter.

"camouflage". *Dictionary.com Unabridged*. Random House, Inc. 18 Jun. 2017.

"bitterness." American Heritage® Dictionary of the English Language, Fifth Edition. 2011. Houghton Mifflin Harcourt Publishing Company 17 Jun. 2017

Smith, Brad. "Hunting Myth Buster: Do You Need Camouflage for Deer Hunting?" *Wide Open Spaces*. N.p., 19 Sept. 2015. Web. 17 Mar. 2017.

"holding pattern." American Heritage® Dictionary of the English

Language, Fifth Edition. 2011. Houghton Mifflin Harcourt Publishing

Company 16 May. 2017

Pinilis, Loren. "A Biblical View of Time: Shifting from Chronos to Kairos." *Life of a Steward*. Christian Time Management, 2012. Web. 2 Apr. 2017.

Badu, Erykah. *Bag Lady*. Universal Motown Records, 2000. MP3.

Mercola, Joseph. "What Happens During a Heart Attack." *Mercola.com*. N.p., 1997-2017. Web. 5 Feb. 2017. <http://articles.mercola.com/heart-attack-symptoms.aspx>.

Evans, Tony. "Preparing Hearts for Destiny."
        Received by Brittany Jenkins, 26 April 2017

CBN.com. "What Does the Bible Say about Bitterness and Resentment?" *CBN.com (beta)*. N.p., 23 Dec. 2015. Web. 23 Apr. 2017. <http://www1.cbn.com/teachingsheets/bible-bitterness-and-resentment>.

Scripture quotations marked (MSG) are taken from The Message Bible. *The Message: The Bible in Contemporary Language*. Large Print Numbered Edition Vers. Colorado Springs: NavPress, 2005. Print.

Scripture quotations marked (NLT) are taken from the Life Application Study Bible *Life Application Study Bible (NLT)*. Carol Stream: Tyndale House, 1988, 1989, 1990, 1991, 1993, 1996, 2004, 2005. Print.

Scripture quotations marked (KJV) are taken from The King James Study Bible. *The King James Study Bible.* Second Vers. N.p.: Thomas Nelson and Livingstone Corporation, 1988, 2013. Print.

Scripture quotations marked (AMP) are taken from the Amplified Study Bible. *Amplified Study Bible.* Grand Rapids: Zondervan, 2016. Print.

Scripture quotations marked (NIV) are taken from The Holy Bible, New International Version. *The Holy Bible, New International Version, NIV.* Grand Rapids: Zondervan, 1985, 2011. Print.

www.ingramcontent.com/pod-product-compliance
Lightning Source LLC
Chambersburg PA
CBHW032041090426
42744CB00004B/83